SIMPLY CAKES

SIMPLY CAKES

Angel, Pound, and Chiffon

ELIZABETH ALSTON

HarperCollins*Publishers*

HarperCollins books may be purchased for educational, business, or sales promotional use. For information, please write: Special Markets Department, HarperCollins Publishers, Inc., 10 East 53rd Street, New York, NY 10022.

FIRST EDITION

Based on a design by Cassandra J. Pappas

Library of Congress Cataloging-in-Publication Data

Alston, Elizabeth.
    Simply cakes : angel, pound, and chiffon / Elizabeth Alston. — 1st ed.
        p.   cm.
    Includes index.
    ISBN 0-06-016988-5
    1. Cake. I. Title.
TX771.A493   1994
641.8'653—dc20   93-26351

94 95 96 97 98 ❖/RRD 10 9 8 7 6 5 4 3 2 1

CONTENTS

ACKNOWLEDGMENTS

With heartfelt thanks to Mary Adams, Rebecca Adams, Louise Burbidge, Dionisia Colon, Ruth Cousineau, Sandra Robishaw, and Miriam Rubin. For word processing: Maria di Martino and Nichelle Gainer.

SIMPLY CAKES

INTRODUCTION

When I was a child, Monday was wash day (and there was baked rice pudding for lunch), Wednesday was market day (which might include an illicit trip to the movies, but definitely meant there'd be fresh fish for dinner). Friday was silver-cleaning day, but Thursday was baking day. Early in the morning, butter was put on the back of the AGA range to soften. I might be sent with a basket to the farm cottage for eggs from our hens. Out came the sugar, the spices, and the flour, the big yellow bowls, the rickety cooling rack, and the kitchen scale (with its big iron weights, the brass 2-ounce weight, and various coins for weighing less than that). In due course, the softened butter was beaten, eggs cracked open, flour sifted, raisins sorted, batters whisked or stirred. Into the well-worn cake pans, lined with freshly cut grease-proof paper, went the creamy yellow batters, studded perhaps with candied cherries or dried fruit. (Small helpers might get a bowl to lick clean.) Soon delicious baking smells wafted through the house, as Victoria sandwich cake (translation: pound cake), sticky gingerbread, sponge cake, Swiss roll (jelly roll), and one or two small cakes (mother's repertoire included rock buns, ragged robins, melting moments, fairy cakes, shortbread, and Aunt Peggy's gypsy creams) were baked for the week ahead. By four o'clock, the old cookie tins in the pantry were filled with new treasures—which of course we weren't supposed to touch, except at the appointed hours!

The output of the weekly baking varied, depending on the season and how many of us four children were home. It was considered essential to have plenty of baked goods on hand to fill up the family, as well as to offer to visitors with a cup of tea or coffee. (A busy farm can expect drop-in visitors, from a neighboring farmer to the veterinarian, at almost any time.)

Today few of us have the need to do a major weekly baking, but a homemade cake tastes just as special as it did then and is, as you will discover, not at all hard to make.

There are many occasions when a cake, rather than something individual like a cookie or muffin, seems called for. A homemade cake makes any occasion memorable and will be miles ahead in flavor of just about any store-bought cake.

In this book I have concentrated on:

ANGEL FOOD CAKES

These delicate cakes are virtually fat-free, and because they are made from only the white part of the egg, they contain no cholesterol. Do not expect to end up with the high-and-haughty look of a bakery cake or one made from a mix. I decided to go for intense flavors, and once you start loading angel food cake batter with (heavy) flavoring ingredients, you lose volume. But I think you'll agree that the results are worth it. Turn to page 17 for a look at the angels. A simple one to try first is Brown Sugar Angel Food Cake, page 20.

POUND CAKES

Rich and smooth, with a fine crumb, pound cakes have a sweet, buttery flavor that comes from lots of butter and sugar.

They keep especially well, so why not make two while you have the ingredients out. Pound cakes begin on page 51. A good one to start with is Miriam's Sour Cream Pound Cake, page 58.

CHIFFON CAKES

These also contain fat but in the form of oil. Most of the ingredients are stirred together (or beaten with an electric mixer). The egg whites are stiffly beaten, then folded in just before baking. Chiffon cakes start on page 95.

There are no frosting recipes here because they are unnecessary. They add only extra work and calories. Instead, I have included a selection of delicious toppings, ranging from heavenly Nutmeg-Honey Whipped Cream (page 118) to Caramel Apples (page 122). There's also a Superb Chocolate Sauce (page 123). A slice of cake with a spoonful of sauce alongside is more enjoyable and, to me, seems more stylish and contemporary than a frosted cake.

When a cake does seem bare on top, sift confectioners' sugar over it with a sugar dredger. Keep a filled dredger handy. It looks like a tin can with a handle on the side and holes in the top and can be found at cookware shops.

INGREDIENTS

FLOUR

While any grain (including oats, barley, rice, and rye) *can* be ground into flour, when we say "flour" we mean wheat flour. Few other "flours" are widely available and all bake *very* differently from wheat flour. That's because wheat contains a high proportion of gluten, a protein component that, when the flour is mixed with water (and no fat or little fat) and beaten or kneaded, develops a stretchy, elastic quality that's just what you need to make wonderful bread.

Flour varies in its gluten content, depending on the variety of wheat from which it is ground. For most cakes, the less gluten—and the less the gluten is developed in the mixing process—the more tender the finished cake. All-purpose flour is "middle-of-the-road" flour. Widely available, it is perfectly fine for both bread and cakes. And it may be the only flour you have on hand when the urge to bake a cake strikes. But you may wish to try cake flour, which contains less gluten, and see if you prefer the softer, finer texture it produces in a cake.

Whole Wheat Flour

I rarely liked the earthy, slightly bitter aftertaste of cakes made with whole wheat flour—until I tasted cakes made with whole white wheat flour. Most of the wheat grown in this country is red wheat, but white wheat (and flour ground from it) is gradually becoming available. It gives you the higher nutritional value of whole wheat but with a very mild flavor.

Sugar

Four kinds of sugar are used in this book: granulated white sugar, confectioners' sugar (granulated sugar in powder form), store-bought brown sugar, and homemade brown sugar.

The brown sugar you buy is made by adding a small amount of molasses to granulated white sugar, which is refined from sugarcane or sugar beet. We all know from experience that brown sugar will form rocklike lumps with the slightest provocation. Even a freshly opened package contains tiny lumps, which, while fine to use in most baking, can leave pockets in an angel food cake unless you sift out the lumps. Sifting brown sugar through a strainer (don't try it with a flour sifter) is time-consuming; once sifted, it starts to form a crust if the sugar stands in dry air for even as little as 10 minutes.

However, angel food cakes made with brown sugar have a rich and wonderful flavor. After spending too much time pushing brown sugar through a strainer it occurred to me to add the molasses and granulated white sugar separately.

Here's how: Regular granulated white sugar is beaten into the egg whites in the usual way, as for white angel food cakes. Then, just before the flour is added, a small amount of molasses is beaten in, essentially creating brown sugar right in the batter.

You can make this change in any recipe using the following quantities as a guide. Use mild or dark (sometimes called robust) molasses, not blackstrap molasses, which is too bitter.

INSTEAD OF	USE
1 cup brown sugar	1 cup granulated white sugar + 2 tablespoons molasses
1¼ cups brown sugar	1¼ cups sugar + 3 tablespoons molasses
1½ cups brown sugar	1½ cups sugar + ¼ cup molasses

Confectioners' sugar may be used instead of regular granulated white sugar in many cakes, and it imparts a more delicate texture (partly due to the small amount of cornstarch it contains). Usually, 2 cups unsifted confectioners' sugar can replace 1 cup granulated white sugar.

BUTTER

For cakes I prefer the fresher flavor of unsalted butter. If you use lightly salted butter, reduce or eliminate any salt in the recipe. You may also use margarine, but please use regular stick margarine or butter. Butter/margarine blends in stick form probably would work well, too, but the recipes haven't been tried with them or with "whipped" or "light" or "diet" butter or margarine, often called "spread."

EGGS

You may use a cholesterol-free egg substitute instead of whole eggs. (Check the packages of individual brands for amounts.) You may also use 2 egg whites instead of 1 whole egg.

Eggs are incorporated more easily into a butter-sugar mixture if they are at room temperature. If you are in a hurry, take the eggs from the refrigerator and put them, *still in the shell*, in a bowl of warm water. After a couple of minutes replace the water with warmer water. Even just 10 minutes in warm water will take the chill out of the eggs.

HOW TO SEPARATE EGG WHITES FROM YOLKS

Angel food cakes use only egg whites, while most chiffon cakes use yolks and whites, but the whites are whipped separately and folded into the batter.

When egg whites are to be stiffly beaten, make sure that the beaters as well as all bowls and containers they will come into contact with are clean, dry, and free from any grease. Even tiny amounts of oil or grease will prevent the whites from mounding properly.

Have at hand the bowl in which the whites will be beaten, plus a custard cup or other small dish (and another container for the yolks, if you're saving them). If you're separating the eggs for an angel food cake, you'll also need a 2-cup glass measure.

Take the eggs straight from the refrigerator (eggs separate most easily when cold). Give 1 egg a sharp rap on the edge of a bowl to break it open. Hold it over the custard cup and gently pull apart the two halves of the shell, letting the yolk slide into one half of the shell, and the egg white drop into the custard cup. Carefully slip the yolk into the other half of the shell; if there is still a lot of white clinging to the yolk, slip it back into the other half shell. Then put the yolk into the container you selected for it, or throw it away.

Pour the whites into the cup measure (or into the bowl in which you will beat them). Then continue separating eggs until you have as much as the recipe calls for. The chalazae, the tiny white spiral bands that anchor the yolk, can go in with the whites or not. Should there be a piece of shell in the whites, fish it out. Fish out any specks of yolk, too, using the edge of a shell or a teaspoon. However, if you break the yolk and a lot of it falls into the white, start again. Because if there's even a small amount of yolk in the whites they will not beat to their full potential. (You can scramble the broken egg for breakfast.)

It takes 10 to 12 "large" eggs to end up with 1½ cups of egg whites.

When you have the desired amount of whites, pour them into the bowl in which you will be beating them. Let them come to room temperature while you assemble the remaining ingredients and tools. (If the whites are still very cold when you are ready to beat them, don't worry. The volume will be only very slightly reduced.)

Nuts

Nuts taste bitter and acrid when they have turned rancid and are not good for you or the cake. Buy from a source that has a fast turnover and/or that sells nuts in sealed bags.

Once you have opened a sealed package, transfer any unused nuts to an airtight container or a heavy-duty plastic bag specifically designed for freezing food. You can use the nuts straight from the freezer.

TO TOAST NUTS

Heat the oven. You can use any temperature ranging from 325°F. up to 375°F. At 375°F., the nuts toast faster and you should not wander far from the kitchen. At 325°F., toasting is more leisurely. Spread the nuts out on a baking pan with sides. Set a timer and bake 8 to 10 minutes, or up to 15 minutes at 325°F., shaking the pan once or twice. The nuts are done when they smell toasted and have changed color slightly. The skins of hazelnuts will have split some. Wrap the hot hazelnuts in a dish towel and rub them together with the towel to loosen the skins, then pick out the nuts. (Some skins will cling tenaciously to the nuts and it is fine to use those nuts.)

BAKING POWDER AND BAKING SODA

These are not the same and can not be used interchangeably. Baking soda is pure bicarbonate of soda. In conjunction with an acidic liquid such as yogurt or buttermilk, it is sometimes the only leavening agent in a cake (but more likely in a biscuit or scone).

Baking soda is usually used in recipes to neutralize the acid found in such ingredients as honey, cocoa, or brown sugar.

Baking powder, on the other hand, is used as a leavening, or raising, agent. *Double-acting baking powder* contains two leavens. One starts to create bubbles when moistened while the other doesn't start to work until heated. The bubbles form and work their way through the batter. As the batter heats and firms, the bubbles are baked in, creating a cake with an open, light texture.

The recipes in this book were tested with double-acting baking powder.

CREAM OF TARTAR

Look for cream of tartar (potassium acid tartrate) in the spice section of your market. It isn't a spice but it is packaged by spice companies in the same small jars or tins.

Cream of tartar is often called for in recipes where egg whites are stiffly beaten because it stabilizes the egg white foam. I use it in angel food cakes because the volume of the finished cake *depends* on the volume of the beaten whites.

EQUIPMENT

BAKING PANS

Baking pans of any kind work fine, but if you need to buy a pan, go for good, basic light-colored aluminum. Cakes brown faster in darker pans, sometimes turning too brown before they are cooked. A nonstick coating makes no sense for a cake baking pan, since it still has to be greased and some of the coating inevitably gets scraped off each time you loosen a cake with a knife. (Even when scratched the pan will still bake okay.) Nonstick or release finishes that are part of the material (and not a "coating") work better, but you still need to grease them. Pans are measured across the inside top. When a loaf pan is called for, I usually specify $9 \times 5 \times 3$ inches. Depending on the manufacturer, any measurements you are lucky enough to find embossed in a pan may not match those given above, but should come close. For example, there's no problem using a pan $9 \times 5 \times 2\frac{3}{4}$ inches or even $8\frac{3}{4} \times 4\frac{3}{4} \times 2\frac{3}{4}$ inches instead. A better way to measure a pan, except one with a removable bottom, is to fill it with a measured amount of water. In most recipes I've given the approximate yield of the batter (taken immediately after mixing, before any baking powder really gets going). This will enable you to decide if an alternate pan size is suitable. (You may wish to bake the batter in miniature loaf pans, or even muffin cups.) As a general guide, whatever pan you choose, fill it no more than half to two-thirds full. (Bake any extra batter in a miniature loaf pan, custard cup, or muffin pan; baking time will be considerably less.)

Use the following as a guide in choosing alternate pans:

PAN DIMENSIONS	APPROXIMATE CAPACITY	MAXIMUM BATTER*
10 × 3-inch round	16 cups	8 cups
10 × 4-inch angel food or tube pan	16 cups	8 cups
9 × 4½-inch Bundt, kugelhopf, or Turk's head	12 cups	6–8 cups
9 × 5 × 3-inch loaf pan	8 cups	5 cups
8½ × 4½ × 2¾-inch loaf pan	6½ cups	4 cups

*Unless recipe specifies otherwise.

Do not bake angel food cakes in Bundt, kugelhopf, or Turk's head pans because it is extremely difficult to get them out.

GREASING PANS

You may use a cooking spray (but not the kind that contains oil and flour, since it builds up a sticky coating). Or you may dip a piece of paper towel in oil or melted butter and wipe a thin layer over the inside of the pan. If you bake often, keep a small glass jar or other microwavable container in the refrigerator with some butter in it, ready for melting and greasing. (Keep the jar covered between uses so the butter doesn't pick up refrigerator aromas.)

ELECTRIC MIXER

For such cakes as pound cakes, which have a large amount of "heavy" batter, use a "stand" electric mixer (comes with its own stand), or a portable electric mixer that's strong enough to handle cookie dough. For angel food cakes, portable mixers are at least as good as a stand mixer because you can move the beaters around the bowl while beating the whites, which makes for more evenly beaten whites and is often faster, too.

FOOD PROCESSOR

Several of the pound cake recipes include food processor methods. You need an 8-cup or larger work bowl to hold all the batter. (To measure: Remove blade, tape hole, fill work bowl with measured cups of sugar.)

TECHNIQUES

MEASURING INGREDIENTS

Correct measuring is important to successful baking. Use *dry-measure* cups (the kind that come in graduated stacks) for measuring dry ingredients such as flour, nuts, and raisins. Use *glass cup measures* (1 cup or larger) for liquids. To measure liquids, place measuring cup on counter, pour in the liquid, and bend over and check the amount at eye level. Use either kind of cup for semisolids such as yogurt or sour cream.

Flour, confectioners' sugar. Use exact-size dry-measure cups. When measuring ¾ cup, for example, use a ½ cup measure and a ¼ cup measure. If a recipe calls for ⅔ cup, fill the

⅓ cup measure twice (unless you have a ⅔ cup measure). Spoon flour (or other powdery ingredients such as confectioners' sugar) into the correct-size cups until overflowing. Draw a metal spatula (or other straight edge) across the top, sweeping off excess. Do not press the flour down in the cup or tap the cup measure on the counter. Either can add considerably more flour than needed.

Granulated sugar. Scoop from the bag or the canister using exact-size dry-measure cups. Level off excess.

Brown sugar. Pack brown sugar firmly into exact-size, dry-measure cups until even with the top.

Spices, baking powder, baking soda. Dip the exact-size measuring spoons into the can or jar (or if the neck of the jar is too narrow to get the spoon in, fill spoons to overflowing over a small piece of wax paper), then sweep off excess with the edge of a metal spatula.

To measure ⅛ teaspoon, measure ¼ teaspoon, then "cut" through the middle with the point of a knife and push off the unneeded ⅛ teaspoon.

HOW TO TELL WHEN A CAKE IS DONE

Even very experienced bakers may hesitate when deciding just when a cake is ready to come out of the oven. The time it takes to bake depends on how warm or cold the ingredients were and, therefore, the starting temperature of the batter; also important are the shape and size of the pan and the material it is made from, and the oven itself. (Each of the five ovens in the *Woman's Day* Test Kitchens bakes slightly differently. One, for example, browns cakes noticeably faster than the others.)

You, the baker, are in charge. Use the time given in a recipe as a guide. Set your timer (one with a long, loud ring) for the shorter amount of time in a range—or even 5 minutes less the first time you make a recipe. When the timer goes off, look carefully at the cake. It should *look* cooked: no wet patches in the middle (or in the surface cracks). When you *touch* the center, your finger should not sink into uncooked batter. A cooked cake springs back when you touch it. The cake should also *smell* cooked and should be just coming away from the sides of the pan. If those signals seem to indicate "cooked," insert a cake tester—a metal wire on a handle—into the center of the cake. It should come out "clean," that is, without any uncooked batter clinging to it. (You may use a toothpick or bamboo skewer instead of a cake tester, but because it leaves smaller holes, a cake tester is best for an angel food cake.)

Removing the Cake from a Pan

Angel food cake should cool completely in the pan, usually turned upside down on a cooling rack. Most pound cakes cool for about 30 minutes in the pan (longer won't hurt) on a cooling rack. This is so the cake can finish baking (in its own heat) and the structure can become firm. Chiffon cakes vary; follow the individual recipe.

Before turning a cake out of the pan, loosen the edges by drawing a thin knife or metal spatula (my baking friends favor an *offset* metal spatula—with the blade at an angle) all around the cake, between the cake and the pan.

Then turn the pan upside down over the cooling rack. The cake should fall out. If it does not, go around the edges again.

More drastic measures should rarely be needed, but if they are, hold the pan (use pot holders) over a gas or electric burner on your stove and rotate the pan just enough to heat the bottom. The heat softens the fat you used to grease the pan and also creates steam that helps free the cake. It's not that easy to heat just the bottom of a pan, but it usually does the trick.

Once the cake is out of the pan, let it cool completely before covering it.

Storing

The flavor of most cakes mellows and deepens if you can leave them for several hours (up to 1 day) at room temperature. When cool, put the cake in an airtight container, seal it in a zip-closure plastic bag, or wrap it carefully in plastic wrap and/or aluminum foil to keep it from drying out.

When freezing a cake, be sure it is well protected. Use plastic zip-closure bags that are specifically for freezing food (and are therefore made of thicker plastic).

Cakes take only a very short time to thaw. Pound cakes can be sliced while still frozen, and thus will thaw even more quickly.

Cutting Cakes

Cut cakes with a light, sawing motion. A very sharp knife with a thin blade works well, as does a serrated knife. The important thing is not to press down hard while cutting angel food or chiffon cakes.

Baking amid Chaos

Phone calls, kids asking questions, and other distractions make it hard to remember whether or not you have already put the baking powder in the mixture and if you measured

1½ cups of flour or 2½ cups. Here's how to help yourself.

Have *lots* of measuring cups and spoons available (yard sales are often a good source). Take the spoons off their ring; keep them handy in a pot on the kitchen counter.

When you are inspired to bake, quickly read through the recipe, making sure you have not only every ingredient, but enough of each.

Before you start mixing the batter, measure every ingredient and leave them in their measuring cup or spoon. (Butter you can leave in the wrapper.) For example, 2½ teaspoons baking powder would occupy two 1-teaspoon measures and one ½-teaspoon measure. (If you don't have enough spoons to do this, put measured baking powder in little heaps on a piece of wax paper so you can easily see you have measured correctly.) If you get distracted, you'll know where you are.

When you have mixed the batter and have put the cake in the oven, immediately set at least one timer and also immediately write down the time you put the cake in. Then, if the timer goes off and you don't hear it, you can at least figure out how long the cake has been baking.

Buy timers with long, loud rings. The kind that you can clip on your belt or hang around your neck may be helpful.

Once you are familiar with a recipe or a technique, prepare a shorthand version. Write the ingredients in black felt pen on a sheet of paper or a large index card. Add an abbreviated version of the instructions. Note the pan size, oven temperature, and baking time. Make one or more photocopies. Tape one inside a kitchen cupboard door, ready for quick reference; file the other.

ANGEL FOOD CAKES

Each time I make an angel food cake I'm amazed at how few ingredients are required and how little time it takes to prepare the batter.

Traditionally, angel food cakes are baked in a tube pan—a tall, slope-sided pan with a hollow tube up the center. However, bakeries often bake angel food cakes in loaf pans. In their book *New Orleans*, Lee Bailey and Ella Brennan call for a plain round 10 × 3-inch pan. My first thought was—a mistake! But the photograph showed a cake with no hole in the middle, which convinced me to try the pan called for. I liked the result very much. It looks more like a regular cake, and more contemporary than a tube-pan cake. Here, the choice is yours. The pan, by the way, can be more than 3 inches high (as a springform pan, for example, commonly is). It just shouldn't be less, because although the finished cake will be only about 2 to 3 inches high, the batter often rises higher than that during baking. Most of the angel food cakes in this book can also be baked in a 9-inch springform pan. This works fine but, because the batter will be deeper, you will need to count on 5 to 10 minutes additional baking time.

Here's a plan of action for angel food cakes:

- Make sure you have all the ingredients and tools you will need.
- Make sure the bowl in which you plan to make the batter

is absolutely clean and grease-free (the beaters, too). Use a metal or glass bowl, not a plastic bowl.

• Take the eggs out of the refrigerator and separate the yolks from the whites (see page 7). You won't need the yolks. Put the whites in the bowl in which you plan to make the batter.

• Turn on the oven, first checking that one rack is in the middle position. Prepare the pan (if any preparation is needed).

• Measure all ingredients and have all tools at hand.

• Start making the batter and do not stop until the cake is in the oven.

• Beat the whites at medium speed and *not* until they are as stiff as possible. To test, lift some of the whites out with a spatula. A long tip should pull out where you lifted from. When properly beaten, the long tip of beaten whites should flop over, not stand stiffly upright. (If too stiff, however, just continue with the recipe. It will be a little tricky to fold in the flour mixture and the volume will be slightly less, but the flavor won't be affected.)

• When the cake tests done, let it cool, upside down, on a cooling rack for at least 1 hour. (Several hours is fine, if more convenient.)

Although the techniques are essentially the same, almost every cake has been written as a separate recipe, because I hate trying to figure out "variations" as much as anyone.

BROWN SUGAR
ANGEL FOOD CAKE

Enjoy the deep, rich flavor alone, or with a small scoop of vanilla or butter pecan ice cream (try mango sorbet in the summertime).

1½ cups egg whites (see page 7 if you need help)
1¼ cups granulated sugar
1¼ cups cake flour, or 1 cup all-purpose flour
1½ teaspoons cream of tartar
⅓ cup mild or dark molasses
Confectioners' sugar (optional)

A 10 x 4-INCH TUBE PAN OR A 9- TO 10-INCH ROUND CAKE PAN WITH SIDES
AT LEAST 3 INCHES HIGH (A REMOVABLE BOTTOM IS HELPFUL)

Check that one rack is in the middle of the oven and heat the oven to 325°F.

Pour the egg whites into the bowl in which you will be making the batter.

If the pan has a removable bottom, do nothing to it. If it does not, lightly butter the bottom (page 11). Line the bottom with wax paper or parchment paper cut to fit, and lightly butter the paper.

Thoroughly mix ¼ cup of the sugar and the flour in a small bowl. Have all ingredients and tools at hand.

Beat the egg whites with an electric mixer on medium speed for about 2 minutes, until frothy and well broken up. Add the cream of tartar and increase speed to medium-high. Beat until the whites lose their yellow cast, greatly increase in volume, and start to turn white.

With the mixer running, slowly sprinkle the remaining 1 cup sugar over the whites. Beat until the whites become very thick, very glossy, and white, and the beaters leave a deep trail. Depending on the mixer, this need only take about 3 minutes total.

Reduce the speed to the lowest possible. Pour in the molasses. Beat a few seconds, scraping the sides of the bowl with a rubber spatula to make sure all the molasses is incorporated.

Quickly sprinkle the flour-sugar mixture over the whites. As soon as it is all added but not completely mixed in, stop the machine and remove the bowl.

With a rubber spatula or a large metal spoon, complete mixing in the flour by folding or gently stirring. Stop just as soon as the flour seems blended in.

With a rubber spatula, scrape the batter (9 to 10 cups) into the pan and spread evenly. Inscribe a circle deep in the batter to release any large air bubbles.

Bake until no moist patches remain in the surface cracks, the cake springs back when touched, and a cake tester inserted in the center comes out clean—about 50 minutes for a 10 × 3-inch pan, 1 hour for a tube pan. Turn the cake pan upside down on a wire rack. Let cool completely.

(continued)

Loosen the edges (and tube) with a knife. Turn out the cake, loosen and remove the pan bottom, or peel off the paper. Store airtight 1 day at room temperature before serving or freezing. If you wish, sift confectioners' sugar over the top before serving.

VARIATION

SPICY BROWN SUGAR ANGEL FOOD CAKE

An excellent everyday cake that can even put in a welcome appearance at a late breakfast. It doesn't *need* a sauce, but for a special occasion such as Thanksgiving, try Nutmeg-Honey Whipped Cream (page 118), Caramel Apples (page 122), or Pineapple–Golden Raisin Sauce (page 119).

Use the same ingredients and pan as for Brown Sugar Angel Food Cake (page 20), plus:

1 teaspoon ground cinnamon
½ teaspoon ground nutmeg
½ teaspoon ground cloves

Follow the directions for Brown Sugar Angel Food Cake, adding the spices to the egg whites while you're adding the last spoonful or two of sugar. Proceed and bake as directed.

FRESH RASPBERRY
ANGEL FOOD CAKE

Enjoy this unbelievably good cake with cappuccino or tea and no other distractions. This cake is best served the day it is made, but if you're keeping it longer, wrap it tightly and refrigerate it.

1½ cups egg whites (see page 7 if you need help)
2 cups (1 pint) fresh red raspberries
1½ cups granulated sugar
1¼ cups cake flour, or 1 cup all-purpose flour
1½ teaspoons cream of tartar
½ cup mild or dark molasses

A 10 x 4-INCH TUBE PAN OR A 9- TO 10-INCH ROUND CAKE PAN WITH SIDES
AT LEAST 3 INCHES HIGH (A REMOVABLE BOTTOM IS HELPFUL)

Check that one rack is in the middle of the oven and heat the oven to 325°F.

Pour the egg whites into the bowl in which you will be making the batter.

If the pan has a removable bottom, do nothing to it. If it does not, lightly butter the bottom (page 11). Line the bottom with wax paper or parchment paper cut to fit, and lightly butter the paper.

(continued)

Do not wash the raspberries, just pick out any very squashed or (of course) moldy ones.

Thoroughly mix ½ cup of the sugar and the flour in a small bowl. Have all ingredients and tools at hand.

Beat the egg whites with an electric mixer on medium speed for about 2 minutes, until frothy and well broken up. Add the cream of tartar and increase speed to medium-high. Beat until the whites lose their yellow cast, greatly increase in volume, and start to turn white.

With the mixer running, slowly sprinkle the remaining 1 cup sugar over the whites. Beat until the whites become very thick, very glossy, and white, and the beaters leave a deep trail. Depending on the mixer, this need only take about 3 minutes total.

Reduce the speed to the lowest possible. Pour in the molasses. Beat a few seconds, scraping the sides of the bowl with a rubber spatula to make sure all the molasses is incorporated.

Quickly sprinkle the flour-sugar mixture over the whites, beating lightly. As soon as it is all added but not completely mixed in, stop the machine and remove the bowl.

Sprinkle the raspberries over the batter. With a rubber spatula or a large metal spoon, complete mixing in the flour along with the raspberries by folding or gently stirring. Stop just as soon as the flour seems blended in.

With a rubber spatula, scrape the batter (9 to 10 cups) into the pan and spread evenly. Inscribe a circle deep in the batter to release any large air bubbles.

Bake until no moist patches remain in the surface cracks, the cake springs back when touched, and a cake tester

inserted in the center comes out clean—about 50 minutes for a 10 × 3-inch pan, 1 hour for a tube pan. Turn the cake pan upside down on a wire rack. Let cool completely.

Loosen the edges (and tube) with a knife. Turn out the cake, loosen and remove the pan bottom, or peel off the paper.

CARAMEL-COFFEE
ANGEL FOOD CAKE

12 TO 16 PORTIONS

You can't add nuts to an angel food cake (their oil causes the beaten whites to collapse), but you can put them on the bottom of the pan. They taste wonderful with the cake even though they make cutting it a little tricky. Try serving the cake *nuts down*. Slice it with a sawing motion; when you come to the nuts cut straight down.

1½ cups egg whites (see page 7 if you need help)
½ cup toasted chopped almonds (page 8)
1¼ cups granulated sugar
1 cup all-purpose flour, or 1¼ cups cake flour
1½ teaspoons cream of tartar
1 tablespoon instant coffee powder, preferably espresso
1 teaspoon vanilla extract
⅓ cup mild molasses
Confectioners' sugar

A 9- TO 10-INCH ROUND CAKE PAN WITH SIDES AT LEAST 3 INCHES HIGH

Check that one rack is in the middle of the oven and heat the oven to 325°F.

Pour the egg whites into the bowl in which you will be making the batter.

Lightly butter the bottom of the pan (page 11). Line with

wax paper or parchment paper cut to fit, and lightly butter the paper. Sprinkle the toasted chopped almonds evenly over the bottom of the pan.

Thoroughly mix ¼ cup of the sugar and the flour in a small bowl. Have all ingredients and tools at hand.

Beat the egg whites with an electric mixer on medium speed for about 2 minutes, until frothy and well broken up. Add the cream of tartar and increase the speed to medium-high. Beat until the whites lose their yellow cast, greatly increase in volume, and start to turn white. Add the instant coffee powder and the vanilla.

With the mixer running, slowly sprinkle the remaining 1 cup sugar over the whites. Beat until the whites become very thick, very glossy, and white, and the beaters leave a deep trail. Depending on the mixer, this need only take about 3 minutes total.

Reduce the speed to the lowest possible. Pour in the molasses. Beat a few seconds, scraping the sides of the bowl with a rubber spatula to make sure all the molasses is incorporated.

Quickly sprinkle the flour-sugar mixture over the whites. As soon as it is all added, but not completely mixed in, stop the machine and remove the bowl.

With a rubber spatula or a large metal spoon, complete mixing in the flour by folding or gently stirring. Stop just as soon as the flour seems blended in.

With a rubber spatula, scrape the batter (9 to 10 cups) into the pan over the almonds and spread evenly. Inscribe a circle deep in the batter to release any large air bubbles.

Bake until no moist patches remain in the surface cracks,

the cake springs back when touched, and a cake tester inserted in the center comes out clean, about 50 minutes. Place the pan on a wire rack; *do not turn upside down.* Let cool completely.

Loosen the edges with a knife. Turn the cake out onto a plate (not the rack) and carefully peel off the paper. Put a cake plate over the cake, hold on to both plates, and turn both over together.

Store airtight 1 day at room temperature before serving or freezing. Sift confectioners' sugar over the top before serving.

APRICOT–BROWN SUGAR ANGEL FOOD CAKE

12 TO 16 PORTIONS

For best flavor, use tart dried apricots from California, not the sweet-to-eat Turkish ones.

1½ cups egg whites (see page 7 if you need help)
4 ounces dried apricots (1 cup)
1¼ cups granulated sugar
1 cup all-purpose flour, or 1¼ cups cake flour
1½ teaspoons cream of tartar
1 teaspoon vanilla extract
⅓ cup mild or dark molasses
Confectioners' sugar (optional)

A 10 x 4-INCH TUBE PAN OR A 9- TO 10-INCH ROUND CAKE PAN WITH SIDES
AT LEAST 3 INCHES HIGH (A REMOVABLE BOTTOM IS HELPFUL)

FOOD PROCESSOR

Check that one rack is in the middle of the oven and heat the oven to 325°F.

Pour the egg whites into the bowl in which you will be making the batter.

If the pan has a removable bottom, do nothing to it. If it does not, lightly butter the bottom (page 11). Line the bottom with wax paper or parchment paper cut to fit, and lightly butter the paper.

(continued)

Snip or cut each apricot into 3 or 4 pieces. Finely chop them in a food processor with ¼ cup of the sugar.

Thoroughly mix another ¼ cup of the sugar and the flour in a small bowl. Have all ingredients and tools at hand.

Beat the egg whites with an electric mixer on medium speed for about 2 minutes, until frothy and well broken up. Add the cream of tartar and increase the speed to medium-high. Beat until the whites lose their yellow cast, greatly increase in volume, and start to turn white.

With the mixer running, slowly sprinkle the remaining ¾ cup sugar over the whites. Then add the apricot and sugar mixture. Beat until the whites become very thick, very glossy, and white, and the beaters leave a deep trail. Depending on the mixer, this need only take about 3 minutes total. Beat in the vanilla.

Reduce the speed to the lowest possible. Pour in the molasses. Beat a few seconds, scraping the sides of the bowl with a rubber spatula to make sure all the molasses is incorporated.

Quickly sprinkle the flour-sugar mixture over the whites. As soon as it is all added, but not completely mixed in, stop the machine and remove the bowl.

With a rubber spatula or a large metal spoon, complete mixing in the flour by folding or gently stirring. Stop just as soon as the flour seems blended in.

With a rubber spatula, scrape the batter (10 to 10½ cups) into the pan and spread evenly. Inscribe a circle deep in the batter to release any large air bubbles.

Bake until no moist patches remain in the surface cracks, the cake springs back when touched, and a cake tester

inserted in the center comes out clean—about 50 minutes for a 10 × 3-inch pan, 1 hour for a tube pan. Turn the pan upside down on a wire rack. Let cool completely.

Loosen the edges (and tube) with a knife. Turn out the cake, loosen and remove the pan bottom, or peel off the paper. Store airtight 1 day at room temperature before serving or freezing. If you wish, sift confectioners' sugar over the top before serving.

FRESH GINGER–BROWN SUGAR ANGEL FOOD CAKE

12 TO 16 PORTIONS

1½ cups egg whites (see page 7 if you need help)
Fresh gingerroot
1¼ cups granulated sugar
1 cup all-purpose flour, or 1¼ cups cake flour
1½ teaspoons cream of tartar
2 tablespoons freshly squeezed lemon juice
½ cup mild molasses
Confectioners' sugar (optional)

A 10 x 4-INCH TUBE PAN OR A 9- TO 10-INCH ROUND CAKE PAN WITH SIDES
AT LEAST 3 INCHES HIGH (A REMOVABLE BOTTOM iS HELPFUL)

Check that one rack is in the middle of the oven and heat the oven to 325°F.

Pour the egg whites into the bowl in which you will be making the batter.

If the pan has a removable bottom, do nothing to it. If it does not, lightly butter the bottom (page 11). Line the bottom with wax paper or parchment paper cut to fit, and lightly butter the paper.

Peel an inch or two of the ginger with a vegetable peeler or knife. Using a grater with small v-shapes, grate enough to make 2 tablespoons, lightly pressed down to measure.

Thoroughly mix ¼ cup of the sugar and the flour in a small bowl. Have all ingredients and tools at hand.

Beat the egg whites with an electric mixer on medium speed for about 2 minutes, until frothy and well broken up. Add the cream of tartar and increase the speed to medium-high. Beat until the whites lose their yellow cast, greatly increase in volume, and start to turn white.

With the mixer running, slowly sprinkle the remaining 1 cup sugar over the whites. Beat until the whites become very thick, very glossy, and white, and the beaters leave a deep trail. Depending on the mixer, this need only take about 3 minutes total. Beat in the lemon juice and grated ginger.

Reduce the speed to the lowest possible. Pour in the molasses. Beat a few seconds, scraping the sides of the bowl with a rubber spatula to make sure all the molasses is incorporated.

Quickly sprinkle the flour-sugar mixture over the whites. As soon as it is all added, but not completely mixed in, stop the machine and remove the bowl.

With a rubber spatula or a large metal spoon, complete mixing in the flour by folding or gently stirring. Stop just as soon as the flour seems blended in.

With a rubber spatula, scrape the batter (9 cups) into the pan and spread evenly. Inscribe a circle deep in the batter to release any large air bubbles.

Bake until no moist patches remain in the surface cracks, the cake springs back when touched, and a cake tester inserted in the center comes out clean—about 45 minutes for a 10 × 3-inch pan, 50 minutes for a tube pan. Turn the cake pan upside down on a wire rack. Let cool completely.

(continued)

Loosen the edges (and tube) with a knife. Turn out the cake, loosen and remove the pan bottom, or peel off the paper. Store airtight 1 day at room temperature before serving or freezing. If you wish, sift confectioners' sugar over the top before serving.

WHOLE WHITE WHEAT–BROWN
SUGAR ANGEL FOOD CAKE

12 TO 16 PORTIONS

Whole white wheat flour is just beginning to be widely available, but it is worth searching out because white wheat leaves none of that bitter aftertaste that regular (red) whole wheat does. Try this cake with Superb Chocolate Sauce (page 123), Nutmeg-Honey Whipped Cream (page 118), or Caramel Apples (page 122).

1½ cups egg whites (see page 7 if you need help)
1¼ cups granulated sugar
1 cup whole white wheat flour
1½ teaspoons cream of tartar
1 teaspoon ground cinnamon
1 teaspoon vanilla extract
⅓ cup mild or dark molasses
Confectioners' sugar (optional)

A 10 x 4-INCH TUBE PAN OR A 9- TO 10-INCH ROUND CAKE PAN WITH SIDES AT LEAST 3 INCHES HIGH (A REMOVABLE BOTTOM IS HELPFUL)

Check that one rack is in the middle of the oven and heat the oven to 325°F.

Pour the egg whites into the bowl in which you will be making the batter.

If the pan has a removable bottom, do nothing to it. If it

does not, lightly butter the bottom (page 11). Line the bottom with wax paper or parchment paper cut to fit, and lightly butter the paper.

Thoroughly mix ¼ cup of the sugar and the flour in a small bowl. Have all ingredients and tools at hand.

Beat the egg whites with an electric mixer on medium speed for about 2 minutes, until frothy and well broken up. Add the cream of tartar and increase the speed to medium-high. Beat until the whites lose their yellow cast, greatly increase in volume, and start to turn white.

With the mixer running, slowly sprinkle the remaining 1 cup sugar over the whites. Add the cinnamon and vanilla. Beat until the whites become very thick, very glossy, and white, and the beaters leave a deep trail. Depending on the mixer, this need only take about 3 minutes total.

Reduce the speed to the lowest possible. Pour in the molasses. Beat a few seconds, scraping the sides of the bowl with a rubber spatula to make sure all the molasses is incorporated.

Quickly sprinkle the flour-sugar mixture over the whites. As soon as it is all added, but not completely mixed in, stop the machine and remove the bowl.

With a rubber spatula or a large metal spoon, complete mixing in the flour by folding or gently stirring. Stop just as soon as the flour seems blended in.

With a rubber spatula, scrape the batter (9 cups) into the pan and spread evenly. Inscribe a circle deep in the batter to release any large air bubbles.

Bake until no moist patches remain in the surface cracks, the cake springs back when touched, and a cake tester

inserted in the center comes out clean—about 50 minutes for a 10 × 3-inch pan, 1 hour for a tube pan. Turn the pan upside down on a wire rack. Let cool completely.

Loosen the edges (and tube) with a knife. Turn out the cake, loosen and remove the pan bottom, or peel off the paper. Store airtight 1 day at room temperature before serving or freezing. If you wish, sift confectioners' sugar over the top before serving.

LEMON-VANILLA
ANGEL FOOD CAKE

12 TO 16 PORTIONS

E xcellent with Raspberry-
Blueberry Sauce (page 120) or a scoop of lemon or lime sorbet, or one of the wilder sorbets such as passion fruit. For a
classy dessert, lay a slender wedge of the cake flat on each
plate, place tiny scoops of two or three sorbets alongside, and
decorate with a chocolate twig candy. Sift a little confectioners' sugar over all, including the plate.

1½ cups egg whites (see page 7 if you need help)
1 cup all-purpose flour, or 1¼ cups cake flour
1¼ cups granulated sugar, or 2½ cups confectioners' sugar
1½ teaspoons cream of tartar
3 tablespoons freshly squeezed lemon juice
1 teaspoon vanilla extract
Confectioners' sugar (optional)

A 10 x 4-INCH TUBE PAN OR A 9- TO 10-INCH ROUND CAKE PAN WITH SIDES
AT LEAST 3 INCHES HIGH (A REMOVABLE BOTTOM IS HELPFUL)

Check that one rack is in the middle of the oven and heat
the oven to 325°F.
Pour the egg whites into the bowl in which you will be making the batter.

If the pan has a removable bottom, do nothing to it. If it does not, lightly butter the bottom (page 11). Line the bottom with wax paper or parchment paper cut to fit, and lightly butter the paper.

Thoroughly mix the flour and ¼ cup of the granulated sugar or ½ cup of the confectioners' sugar in a small bowl. Have all ingredients and tools at hand.

Beat the egg whites with an electric mixer on medium speed for about 2 minutes, until frothy and well broken up. Add the cream of tartar and increase the speed to medium-high. Beat until the whites lose their yellow cast, greatly increase in volume, and start to turn white.

With the mixer running, slowly sprinkle the remaining sugar over the whites. Beat until the whites become very thick, very glossy, and white, and the beaters leave a deep trail. Depending on the mixer, this need only take about 3 minutes total. Beat in the lemon juice and vanilla, just enough to mix.

Reduce the speed to the lowest possible. Quickly sprinkle the flour-sugar mixture over the whites. As soon as it is all added, but not completely mixed in, stop the machine and remove the bowl.

With a rubber spatula or a large metal spoon, complete mixing in the flour by folding or gently stirring. Stop just as soon as the flour seems blended in.

With a rubber spatula, scrape the batter (9 cups) into the pan and spread evenly. Inscribe a circle deep in the batter to release any large air bubbles.

Bake until no moist patches remain in the surface cracks, the cake springs back when touched, and a cake tester

inserted in the center comes out clean—about 50 minutes for a 10 × 3-inch pan, 1 hour for a tube pan. Turn the pan upside down on a wire rack. Let cool completely.

Loosen the edges (and tube) with a knife. Turn out the cake, loosen and remove the pan bottom, or peel off the paper. Store airtight 1 day at room temperature before serving or freezing. If you wish, sift confectioners' sugar over the top before serving.

HAZELNUT-CHOCOLATE
ANGEL FOOD CAKE

The combination of hazelnut and chocolate is close to the top of my favorite-flavor chart, but it's hard to achieve in an angel food cake because the oil in nuts causes the beaten egg whites to collapse. The same problem arose with the Caramel-Coffee Angel Food Cake on page 26. The surprisingly simple solution is to sprinkle the nuts on the bottom of the pan, where they form a wonderful toasty crust. True, this makes neat slices a problem, but the flavor is worth it. Put the cake nut-side down on the serving plate, then sprinkle the surface with confectioners' sugar. Cut straight through the nuts with a sharp knife. Because of the lavish amount of cocoa, the cake itself is more like a dense mousse and only about 1½ inches high. Toasted almonds, pecans, or walnuts can be used instead of the hazelnuts.

1½ cups egg whites (see page 7 if you need help)
½ cup toasted chopped hazelnuts (page 8)
1¾ cups granulated sugar
⅔ cup all-purpose flour
⅔ cup unsweetened cocoa powder
1½ teaspoons cream of tartar
1 tablespoon vanilla extract
Confectioners' sugar

(continued)

A 9- TO 10-INCH ROUND CAKE PAN WITH SIDES AT LEAST 3 INCHES HIGH
(A REMOVABLE BOTTOM IS HELPFUL)

Check that one rack is in the middle of the oven and heat the oven to 325°F.

Pour the egg whites into the bowl in which you will be making the batter.

Lightly butter the bottom of the pan (page 11). Line the bottom with wax paper or parchment paper cut to fit, and lightly butter the paper. Sprinkle the toasted chopped hazelnuts evenly over the bottom of the pan.

Thoroughly mix ½ cup of the sugar, the flour, and the cocoa in a small bowl. Have all ingredients and tools at hand.

Beat the egg whites with an electric mixer on medium speed for about 2 minutes, until frothy and well broken up. Add the cream of tartar and increase the speed to medium-high. Beat until the whites lose their yellow cast, greatly increase in volume, and start to turn white.

With the mixer running, slowly sprinkle the remaining 1¼ cups sugar over the whites. Beat until the whites become very thick, very glossy, and white, and the beaters leave a deep trail. Depending on the mixer, this need only take about 3 minutes total. Add the vanilla.

Reduce the speed to the lowest possible. Quickly sprinkle the flour-cocoa mixture over the whites. As soon as it is all added, but not completely mixed in, stop the machine and remove the bowl.

With a rubber spatula or a large metal spoon, complete mixing in the flour by folding or gently stirring. Stop just as soon as the flour seems blended in.

With a rubber spatula, scrape the batter (8 cups) into the pan over the hazelnuts and spread evenly. Inscribe a circle deep in the batter to release any large air bubbles.

Bake until no moist patches remain in the surface cracks, the cake springs back when touched, and a cake tester inserted in the center comes out clean, about 50 minutes. Place the pan on a wire rack; *do not turn upside down.* Let cool completely.

Loosen the edges with a knife. Turn the cake out onto the rack and carefully peel off the paper. Put a cake plate over the cake, hold onto the rack and plate, and turn both over together. Store airtight 1 day at room temperature before serving or freezing. Sift confectioners' sugar over the top before serving.

CAPPUCCINO ANGEL FOOD CAKE

12 TO **16** PORTIONS

$\mathbf{E}$very bite or two you get a tiny crunchy jolt of cinnamon sugar. If you wish, sift 1 tablespoon cocoa or 1 teaspoon cinnamon and 1 tablespoon confectioners' sugar over the cake just before serving.

1½ cups egg whites (see page 7 if you need help)
1¼ cups plus 2 tablespoons granulated sugar
1 cup all-purpose flour
1 teaspoon ground cinnamon
1½ teaspoons cream of tartar
1 tablespoon instant coffee powder or granules,
  preferably espresso

A 9- TO 10-INCH ROUND CAKE PAN WITH SIDES AT LEAST 3 INCHES HIGH OR A
10 x 4-INCH TUBE PAN (A REMOVABLE BOTTOM IS HELPFUL)

Check that one rack is in the middle of the oven and heat the oven to 325°F.

Pour the egg whites into the bowl in which you will be making the batter.

If the pan has a removable bottom, do nothing to it. If it does not, lightly butter the bottom (page 11). Line the bottom with wax paper or parchment paper cut to fit, and lightly butter the paper.

Thoroughly mix ¼ cup of the sugar and the flour in a small

bowl. Mix the 2 tablespoons sugar and the cinnamon in a small dish. Have all ingredients and tools at hand.

Beat the egg whites with an electric mixer on medium speed for about 2 minutes, until frothy and well broken up. Add the cream of tartar and increase the speed to medium-high. Beat until the whites lose their yellow cast, greatly increase in volume, and start to turn white.

With the mixer running, slowly sprinkle the remaining 1 cup sugar over the whites. After 3 or 4 tablespoons, add the coffee powder. Beat until the whites become very thick, very glossy, and pale beige, and the beaters leave a deep trail. Depending on the mixer, this need only take about 3 minutes total.

Reduce the speed to the lowest possible. Quickly sprinkle the flour-sugar mixture over the whites. As soon as it is all added, but not completely mixed in, stop the machine and remove the bowl.

With a rubber spatula or a large metal spoon, complete mixing in the flour by folding or gently stirring. Stop just as soon as the flour seems blended in.

With a rubber spatula, scrape about half the 8 to 9 cups batter in the pan and spread evenly. Sprinkle the cinnamon sugar evenly over the surface. Drop spoonfuls of the remaining batter over the cinnamon sugar and spread fairly evenly. Using the spatula, inscribe a circle deep in the batter to release any large air bubbles.

Bake until no moist patches remain in the surface cracks, the cake springs back when touched, and a cake tester inserted in the center comes out clean, about 50 minutes.

(continued)

Turn the pan upside down on a wire rack. Let cool completely.

Loosen the edges (and tube) with a knife. Turn out the cake, loosen and remove the pan bottom, or peel off the paper. Store airtight 1 day at room temperature before serving or freezing.

PEPPERMINT STICK ANGEL FOOD CAKE

If you love peppermint stick ice cream, you'll love this cake. And if you love mint chocolate chip ice cream even more, try the recipe that follows. A small scoop of ice cream—vanilla or, what the heck, peppermint stick—and/or a spoonful of chocolate sauce make a wedge of either cake into a spectacular dessert.

1½ cups egg whites (see page 7 if you need help)
About 14 round red-and-white peppermint candies
1¼ cups cake flour, or 1 cup all-purpose flour
2½ cups confectioners' sugar, or 1 cup granulated sugar
1½ teaspoons cream of tartar
1 teaspoon vanilla extract
Confectioners' sugar (optional)

A 10 x 4-INCH TUBE PAN OR A 9- TO 10-INCH ROUND CAKE PAN WITH SIDES
AT LEAST 3 INCHES HIGH (A REMOVABLE BOTTOM IS HELPFUL)

Check that one rack is in the middle of the oven and heat the oven to 325°F.

Pour the egg whites into the bowl in which you will be making the batter.

If the pan has a removable bottom, do nothing to it. If it does not, lightly butter the bottom (page 11). Line the bottom with wax paper or parchment paper cut to fit, and lightly butter the paper.

Finely chop the mints in a food processor, or, a few at a time, in a blender. You need ¼ cup.

Thoroughly mix the flour and ½ cup of the confectioners' sugar or ¼ cup granulated sugar in a bowl. Have all ingredients and tools at hand.

Beat the egg whites with an electric mixer on medium speed for about 2 minutes, until frothy and well broken up. Add the cream of tartar and increase the speed to medium-high. Beat until the whites lose their yellow cast, greatly increase in volume, and start to turn white.

With the mixer running, slowly sprinkle the remaining sugar over the whites. Beat until the whites become very thick, very glossy, and white, and the beaters leave a deep trail. Depending on the mixer, this need only take about 3 minutes total. Add the crushed peppermint candy and the vanilla; beat just enough to mix.

Reduce the speed to the lowest possible. Quickly sprinkle the flour-sugar mixture over the whites. As soon as it is all added, but not completely mixed in, stop the machine and remove the bowl. With a rubber spatula or a large metal spoon, complete mixing in the flour by folding or gently stirring. Stop just as soon as the flour seems blended in.

With a rubber spatula, scrape the batter (9 cups) into the pan and spread evenly. Inscribe a circle deep in the batter to release any large air bubbles.

Bake until no moist patches remain in the surface cracks, the cake is light brown and springs back when touched, and a cake tester inserted in the center comes out clean—about 50 minutes for a 10×3-inch pan, 1 hour for a tube pan. Turn the pan upside down on a wire rack. Let cool completely.

Loosen the edges (and tube) with a knife. Remove the pan, loosen and remove the pan bottom, or peel off the paper. Store airtight at room temperature at least 1 day before serving or freezing. If you wish, sift confectioners' sugar over the cake before serving.

VARIATION

SPECKLED CHOCOLATE-MINT ANGEL FOOD CAKE

Use the same ingredients and pan as for Peppermint Stick Angel Food Cake (page 47), plus:

2 ounces bittersweet or semisweet chocolate, finely chopped

You can chop the chocolate by hand, in a food processor, or about one third at a time in a blender.

Follow directions for the Peppermint Stick Angel Food Cake, tossing in the chopped chocolate with the flour-sugar mixture. Proceed and bake as directed.

POUND CAKES

Pound cakes get their name from old recipes that call for a pound each of butter, sugar, and flour. You can vary those proportions considerably and still end up with a cake that has the distinctive sweet, buttery smell and moist, fine texture of a pound cake. (Compared to, say, the more open texture of a coffeecake, which is a shade closer to bread.) A good pound cake has no large holes in it and crumbles when rubbed between your fingers. Pound cakes are made by beating butter and sugar to incorporate air, beating in eggs, and, adding the flour by hand with a wooden spoon or with a mixer on low. While many pound cakes rely totally on the air beaten in to make them rise, I do like to include a small amount of baking powder for insurance.

Here's the plan of action for making a pound cake:
- Check that you have all the ingredients.
- Bring the eggs and the butter to room temperature.
- Turn on the oven.
- Prepare the pan.
- Prepare all other ingredients.
- Make the batter and bake it.

Because of the high proportion of fat in a pound cake, the pan needs only a very light greasing. I prefer to use butter, but vegetable shortening or cooking spray work fine, too.

When *butter* for pound cake is "at room temperature," it is soft enough to beat easily, but not so soft that it is practically melted. Depending on the time available and the temperature of your kitchen you might:

• Leave the butter in its wrapper on the counter for an hour or so.

• Open the butter wrapper and cut as much as you need into small pieces. Leave at room temperature 30 minutes to 1 hour.

• Put the unwrapped butter in a small microwave-safe dish. Microwave in 10-second increments, poking the butter to test it after each 10-second interval, until it is soft. Be very careful! If you melt the butter, start again. Melted butter will not beat up light and fluffy with the sugar.

Eggs for pound cake should be at room temperature, too, to help prevent the butter and sugar mixture from "breaking" or "curdling," that is, breaking into small particles. (If that happens, don't worry about it. You will lose some volume, but it is not a disaster.) To warm eggs quickly, put them, in their shells, in a bowl of very warm water. After 5 minutes or so, pour off the cooled water and add fresh warm water. After 5 to 10 minutes longer, the eggs will be ready to use. Another way is to break all the eggs into a bowl and beat them with a fork. Let them stand 10 to 15 minutes at room temperature, then add them to the mixture about ¼ cup at a time (don't measure, just guess).

Pound cakes can be eaten freshly baked, once they have cooled. But for best flavor, tightly wrap the cooled cake (or put in an airtight container), and let stand 1 day at room temperature for the flavor to develop.

SOUR CREAM AND WALNUT SPICE CAKE

12 PORTIONS

SPICE MIXTURE

1¼ teaspoons ground nutmeg

1 teaspoon ground cinnamon

½ teaspoon ground allspice

¼ teaspoon ground cardamom

CAKE

1 cup plus 4 tablespoons granulated sugar

14 tablespoons (1¾ sticks) unsalted butter,
  at room temperature

2 teaspoons vanilla extract

4 large eggs, at room temperature

¾ cup sour cream

1 teaspoon baking powder

¼ teaspoon baking soda

¼ teaspoon salt

1 cup chopped walnuts

2¼ cups all-purpose flour

A 9 × 5 × 3-INCH LOAF PAN

Heat the oven to 325°F. Grease the pan and line with foil, letting it hang over the sides. Grease the foil.

Mix the spices in a cup. Mix ¼ teaspoon of the spice mixture with 2 tablespoons of the sugar, and set aside to use for the topping.

Beat the butter, the remaining 1 cup plus 2 tablespoons sugar, and the vanilla with an electric mixer on high speed, until pale and fluffy.

Reduce the speed to medium. Add the eggs, 1 at a time, beating after each.

Reduce the mixer speed to low. Stir in the sour cream, the remaining spice mixture, the baking powder, baking soda, and salt. Add the walnuts. Scrape the sides of the bowl often.

With the mixer still on low, stir in the flour just until incorporated. Do not overmix.

Spread the batter (6 cups) in the prepared pan. Sprinkle the reserved sugar-spice mixture over the top. (It will look like too much topping, but it isn't.)

Bake until a cake tester inserted in the center comes out clean, about 1 hour and 10 minutes.

Cool the cake in the pan on a wire rack for about 30 minutes. Lift the cake from the pan by the foil. Let cool completely on the wire rack. Remove the foil. For best flavor, wrap airtight, being careful not to disturb the sugar topping too much, and store 1 day at room temperature before serving or freezing.

SOUR CREAM–CHOCOLATE CHIP POUND CAKE

12 PORTIONS

1 cup plus 4 tablespoons granulated sugar
1½ teaspoons ground cinnamon
14 tablespoons (1¾ sticks) unsalted butter,
  at room temperature
2 teaspoons vanilla extract .
4 large eggs, at room temperature
¾ cup sour cream
1 teaspoon baking powder
¼ teaspoon baking soda
¼ teaspoon salt
2¼ cups all-purpose flour
1½ cups semisweet chocolate chips

A 9 × 5 × 3-INCH LOAF PAN

Heat the oven to 325°F. Grease the pan and line with foil, letting it hang over the sides. Grease the foil.

Mix 2 tablespoons of the sugar with ¼ teaspoon of the cinnamon, and set aside to use for the topping.

Beat the butter, the remaining 1 cup plus 2 tablespoons sugar, and the vanilla with an electric mixer on high speed, until pale and fluffy.

Reduce the speed to medium. Add the eggs, 1 at a time, beating after each.

Beat in the sour cream, baking powder, baking soda, salt, and the remaining 1¼ teaspoons cinnamon. Scrape the sides of the bowl often.

With the mixer on low, stir in the flour until nearly incorporated. Stir in the chocolate chips with a wooden spoon, until the batter is smooth and well mixed.

Spread the batter (6½ cups) in the pan (pan will be very full). Sprinkle the reserved cinnamon sugar over the top. (It will look like too much topping, but it isn't.)

Bake until a cake tester inserted in the center comes out clean, about 1 hour and 10 minutes.

Cool the cake in the pan on a wire rack for about 30 minutes. Lift the cake from the pan by the foil. Let cool completely on the wire rack. Remove the foil. For best flavor, wrap airtight, being careful not to disturb the sugar topping more than necessary, and store 1 day at room temperature before serving or freezing.

MIRIAM'S SOUR CREAM POUND CAKE

12 PORTIONS

In addition to being a great cook, Miriam Rubin is a food writer and editor.

1 cup plus 2 tablespoons granulated sugar, or
*   2 cups confectioners' sugar*
14 tablespoons (1¾ sticks) unsalted butter,
*   at room temperature*
1 tablespoon vanilla extract
4 large eggs, at room temperature
¾ cup sour cream
1 teaspoon baking powder
¼ teaspoon baking soda
¼ teaspoon salt
2¼ cups all-purpose flour, or 2½ cups cake flour
2 tablespoons granulated sugar, for topping

A 9 × 5 × 3-INCH LOAF PAN

Heat the oven to 325°F. Grease the pan and line with foil, letting it hang over the sides. Grease the foil.

Beat the sugar, butter, and vanilla with an electric mixer on high speed, until pale and fluffy.

Reduce the speed to medium. Add the eggs, 1 at a time, beating after each.

Beat in the sour cream, baking powder, baking soda, and salt. Scrape the sides of the bowl often.

With the mixer on low, stir in the flour just until incorporated. Do not overmix.

Spread the batter (5 cups) in the pan. Sprinkle the 2 tablespoons granulated sugar for the topping over the top. (It will look like too much sugar, but it isn't.)

Bake until a cake tester inserted in the center comes out clean, about 1 hour and 10 minutes.

Cool the cake in the pan on a wire rack for about 30 minutes. Lift the cake from the pan by the foil. Let cool completely on the wire rack. Remove the foil. For best flavor, wrap airtight, being careful not to disturb the sugar topping too much, and store 1 day at room temperature before serving or freezing.

HAZELNUT POUND CAKE

Fantastic flavor that improves with time. Good with tea, coffee, or a glass of sherry or dessert wine. Try the easy food processor method, but be sure to use one with a full-size (8 cups or larger) work bowl.

1 cup toasted hazelnuts, (page 8; see Note)
1 cup granulated sugar
16 tablespoons (2 sticks) unsalted butter,
  at room temperature
1 teaspoon vanilla extract
4 large eggs, at room temperature
1 teaspoon baking powder
¼ teaspoon salt
2 cups all-purpose flour, or 2¼ cups cake flour

A 9 × 5 × 3-INCH LOAF PAN

Heat the oven to 325°F. Grease the pan.

Food processor method: Process the hazelnuts and sugar until the nuts are finely chopped, about 30 seconds. Add the butter and vanilla and process about 30 seconds, until pale and creamy.

With the machine still running, add the eggs, 1 at a time. Add the baking powder and salt. Scrape the sides of the bowl.

Sprinkle the flour over the surface. Turn the machine on/off several times, until the mixture is smooth and well blended.

Spread the batter (4 to 5 cups) evenly in the pan. Bake until a cake tester inserted in the center comes out clean, about 1 hour and 20 to 25 minutes.

Cool the cake in the pan on a wire rack for about 30 minutes. Loosen the edges and turn the cake out. Let cool completely. Store airtight at least 1 day at room temperature before serving or freezing.

Electric mixer method: Grind the toasted hazelnuts in a nut mill or in batches in a blender, or chop as fine as possible with a knife. Beat the sugar and butter in a large bowl with an electric mixer on high speed about 5 minutes, until pale and fluffy. Reduce the speed to medium. Add the eggs, 1 at a time, beating after each. Scrape the sides of the bowl often.

Add the hazelnuts, baking powder, salt, and vanilla. Beat to blend well. With the mixer on low, add the flour and mix only until just incorporated. Do not overmix. Bake and store as above.

NOTE: If you can buy hazelnuts already toasted and chopped, simply process them briefly with the sugar.

CARAWAY SEED CAKE

One of my favorites.

2 tablespoons caraway seeds
1 cup granulated sugar
16 tablespoons (2 sticks) unsalted butter,
  at room temperature
4 large eggs, at room temperature
1 teaspoon baking powder
¼ teaspoon salt
2 cups all-purpose flour, or 2¼ cups cake flour

A 9 × 5 × 3-INCH OR AN 8½ × 4½ × 2¾-INCH LOAF PAN

Heat the oven to 325°F. Grease the pan.

Food processor method: Process the caraway seeds and the sugar for 1 to 2 minutes. Let the sugar dust settle before you open the container. The seeds won't turn to powder, but processing does help release the flavor. Add the butter and process about 30 seconds, until pale and creamy.

With the machine still running, add the eggs, 1 at a time. Add the baking powder and salt. Scrape the sides of the bowl. Sprinkle the flour over the surface. Turn the machine on/off several times, until the mixture is smooth and well blended.

Spread the batter (3 to 4 cups) evenly in the pan. Bake until a cake tester inserted in the center comes out clean—about 1 hour and 10 to 15 minutes for the larger pan, close to 1½ hours for the smaller pan.

Cool the cake in the pan on a wire rack for about 30 minutes. Loosen the edges and turn the cake out. Let cool completely. Store airtight 1 to 2 days at room temperature before serving or freezing.

Electric mixer method: Grind the seeds in a nut mill. Or, put ½ cup of the sugar in a blender and sprinkle the seeds on top of the sugar. Blend or grind for 30 to 60 seconds (seeds will break up). Allow the sugar dust to settle before you open the container. Beat the butter and all of the sugar in a large bowl with an electric mixer on high speed about 5 minutes, until pale and fluffy. Reduce the speed to medium. Add the eggs, 1 at a time, beating after each. Scrape the sides of the bowl often. Add the baking powder and salt. Beat to blend well. With the mixer on low, add the flour and mix only until just incorporated. Do not overmix. Bake and store as above.

TENNESSEE WHISKEY CAKE

T his keeps real well in the refrigerator or freezer. Serve thin slices with a small scoop of ice cream or Nutmeg-Honey Whipped Cream (page 118).

1¼ cups pecans
16 tablespoons (2 sticks) unsalted butter,
   at room temperature
¾ cup granulated sugar
½ cup packed dark brown sugar
2 teaspoons vanilla extract
5 large eggs, at room temperature
¼ cup sour-mash whiskey or bourbon
1 teaspoon baking powder
¼ teaspoon baking soda
¼ teaspoon salt
2 cups all-purpose flour, or 2¼ cups cake flour
10 to 16 pecan halves for decoration

A 9 × 3-INCH SPRINGFORM PAN, A 9 × 5 × 3-INCH LOAF PAN,
OR A 10-CUP TUBE PAN

Heat the oven to 400°F. Spread the 1¼ cups pecans on a baking sheet and bake 10 to 15 minutes, stirring occasionally, until toasted and lightly browned. Cool. Grind about half the nuts in a food processor. Add the rest of the toasted nuts and turn the machine on/off three or four times to chop coarsely.

Meanwhile, reduce the oven temperature to 325°F. and grease the pan.

Beat the butter, sugars, and vanilla with an electric mixer on high speed, until light and fluffy.

Reduce the speed to medium. Add the eggs, 1 at a time, beating after each.

Beat in the whiskey or bourbon, the baking powder, baking soda, and salt (batter will look curdled). Stir in the chopped pecans.

With mixer on low, stir in the flour until just incorporated. Do not overmix.

Spread the batter (6 cups) in the prepared pan. Smooth the top with a spatula. Arrange the pecan halves on top of the batter.

Bake until a cake tester inserted in the center comes out clean and the cake is springy to the touch and shrinks from the sides of the pan, about 50 minutes to 1 hour.

Cool the cake in the pan on a wire rack for about 30 minutes. Loosen edges. Turn cake out or remove sides of spring-form pan and with a thin metal spatula, slide cake off metal pan bottom to a wire rack. Let cool completely. For best flavor, store airtight 1 day at room temperature before serving or freezing.

TRIPLE-GINGER POUND CAKE

12 PORTIONS

Each kind of ginger contributes its own special quality to this wonderful mellow cake, studded with flecks of crystallized ginger. Buy crystallized ginger by the pound at candy shops or some specialty food shops. It's much less expensive than buying tiny jars from the supermarket spice section.

3 to 4 ounces fresh gingerroot
2 to 3 ounces crystallized ginger
1 cup granulated sugar
16 tablespoons (2 sticks) unsalted butter,
*   at room temperature*
4 large eggs, at room temperature
1 teaspoon baking powder
½ teaspoon ground ginger
¼ teaspoon salt
2 cups all-purpose flour

A 9 × 5 × 3-INCH LOAF PAN

FOOD PROCESSOR

Heat the oven to 325°F. Grease the pan.

Peel the fresh ginger with a knife or vegetable peeler and coarsely chop enough to make ¼ cup.

Reserve a few pieces of the crystallized ginger to decorate

the top of the cake. Put the fresh ginger and the remaining crystallized ginger in a food processor, along with the sugar. Process 3 to 4 minutes to grind the gingers finely. The sugar will get quite damp.

Add the butter and process about 1 minute, until the mixture is pale and fluffy. With the machine still running, add the eggs, 1 at a time, stopping the machine once to scrape the sides of the bowl.

Add the baking powder, ground ginger, and salt. Process briefly to mix. Scrape the sides of the bowl. Sprinkle the flour over the surface. Turn the machine on/off several times, just until the flour is blended, scraping the sides of the bowl once.

Spread the batter (4 to 5 cups) in the pan. Draw the handle of a rubber spatula once lengthwise through the batter ½ inch deep. (This will bake into an attractive split.)

Slice the reserved crystallized ginger thin, and scatter or arrange on top of the batter. Bake until a cake tester inserted in the center comes out clean, about 1 hour and 25 minutes.

Cool the cake in the pan on a wire rack for 30 to 40 minutes. Loosen the edges and turn out the cake. Let cool completely. Store airtight 1 day at room temperature before serving or freezing.

WALNUT–POPPY SEED
POUND CAKE

16 PORTIONS

The inspiration for this cake was one created by Ilse Loipner, when she was pastry chef at Windows on the World restaurant in New York City. This delicate, beautiful cake is perfect for any occasion, with a glass of dessert wine, French roast coffee, or Earl Grey tea. Try to buy good, fresh poppy seeds from a source with a fast turnover. A store selling Middle European or Middle Eastern groceries is a much better bet (and usually much less expensive) than the little jars or boxes sold in the supermarket spice section, which may have lingered there for years. If you're in a hurry, you can omit toasting the seeds and nuts.

½ cup poppy seeds (3 ounces)
1 cup granulated sugar
1 cup walnuts
16 tablespoons (2 sticks) unsalted butter,
  at room temperature
4 large eggs, at room temperature
1 teaspoon baking powder
1 teaspoon vanilla extract
¼ teaspoon salt
2 cups all-purpose flour

A 9 × 5 × 3-INCH LOAF PAN

Blender and electric mixer method: "Grind" the poppy seeds in a blender for 2 minutes. The seeds will darken but will not turn to powder or paste. Add about ¼ cup of the sugar and "grind" about 1 minute longer. Do not remove the blender lid until the cloud of sugar has settled.

Put a plate or a sheet of foil next to the stovetop. Tip the poppy seed mixture into a heavy skillet, 8 to 9 inches across the bottom. Grind the walnuts in two batches in the blender, and add to the skillet. Stir over moderate heat for 6 to 7 minutes, until seeds and nuts smell toasted. Scrape the hot mixture onto the plate or sheet of foil so it stops cooking. Spread it out and let cool completely. (If the mixture is warm it may melt the butter and a very dense, although still delicious, cake will result.) Set aside about 2 tablespoons of the poppy seed mixture to sprinkle on top of the cake. (This much can be done a day or so ahead; refrigerate the cooled mixture in an airtight container.)

Meanwhile, heat the oven to 325°F. and grease the pan.

Beat the butter and the remaining ¾ cup sugar with an electric mixer on high speed, until pale and fluffy. Add 2 of the eggs, 1 at a time, beating after each. Beat in about half the poppy seed mixture. Beat in the remaining eggs, then the remaining poppy seed mixture. Beat in the baking powder, vanilla, and salt.

With mixer on low, add the flour. Stir just until incorporated. Do not overmix.

Spread the batter (4 to 5 cups) evenly in the pan. Sprinkle with the reserved 2 tablespoons poppy seed mixture. Bake until a cake tester inserted in the center comes out clean, about 1 hour and 5 to 15 minutes.

(continued)

Cool the cake in the pan on a wire rack for about 30 minutes. Loosen the edges and turn the cake out. Let cool completely. Serve freshly baked, or wrap airtight and store up to 5 days at room temperature or freeze.

Food processor method: Process the poppy seeds, ¼ cup of the sugar, and the walnuts in a food processor in the same way as for the blender, then toast in the skillet and cool completely. Process the butter and the remaining ¾ cup sugar for 1 or 2 minutes, until pale and fluffy. With machine running, add the eggs, 1 at a time. Add the baking powder, vanilla, and salt. Process to mix. Reserve 2 tablespoons of the poppy seed mixture for the topping. Add the remaining poppy seed mixture and process briefly to mix. Sprinkle the flour over the surface. Process a few seconds, just to incorporate, scraping sides of bowl once. Bake and store as directed above.

SOAKED ORANGE POUND CAKE

12 PORTIONS

Good with a small glass of orange-flavored liqueur or with lemonade on the porch on a hot summer afternoon.

CAKE

2 medium-sized navel oranges
1 cup granulated sugar, or 2 cups confectioners' sugar
16 tablespoons (2 sticks) unsalted butter,
   at room temperature
1½ teaspoons vanilla extract
4 large eggs, at room temperature
1 teaspoon baking powder
¼ teaspoon salt
2 cups all-purpose flour, or 2¼ cups cake flour

SYRUP

⅓ cup freshly squeezed orange juice (use oranges from cake
   plus additional juice, if needed)
3 tablespoons granulated sugar
2 teaspoons freshly squeezed lemon juice

AN 8- TO 12-CUP TUBE, TURK'S HEAD, OR BUNDT PAN

Heat the oven to 325°F. Grease the pan well.

Scrub and dry the oranges. With a vegetable peeler, remove the brightly colored part of the peel and measure it. You need

⅓ cup packed. Squeeze the oranges and reserve the juice for the syrup.

Put the orange peel and the sugar in a food processor and process until the peel is very finely chopped. (Instead of using a food processor, you may grate the unpeeled orange and add the peel to the sugar in the bowl.) The sugar will be very damp. Scrape the sugar mixture into the bowl in which you plan to make the batter.

Add the butter and vanilla and beat with an electric mixer on high speed, until pale and fluffy.

Reduce the speed to medium. Add the eggs, 1 at a time, beating after each. Beat in the baking powder and salt. Scrape the sides of the bowl often.

With the mixer on low, sprinkle in the flour and stir just until incorporated. Do not overmix.

Spread the batter (6 cups) evenly in the pan. Bake until a cake tester inserted in the center comes out clean, about 55 minutes to 1 hour and 5 minutes.

Meanwhile, mix the syrup ingredients in a small saucepan, and stir over moderately high heat until the sugar is dissolved and the syrup is hot. Remove from the heat.

Cool the cake in the pan on a wire rack for 10 minutes. Poke about 36 holes in the cake with a long bamboo or metal skewer. Brush the cake with all but about 1 tablespoon of the warm syrup. The surface will look quite wet. Let stand 10 to 15 minutes. Loosen the edges and turn the cake out. Let cool completely. Brush with the remaining 1 tablespoon orange syrup. For best flavor, store airtight 1 day at room temperature before serving or freezing.

ORANGE–CHOCOLATE CHUNK POUND CAKE

12 PORTIONS

3¼ to 4 ounces bittersweet or semisweet chocolate
2 medium-sized navel oranges
1 cup granulated sugar
16 tablespoons (2 sticks) unsalted butter,
  at room temperature
1½ teaspoons vanilla extract
4 large eggs, at room temperature
1 teaspoon baking powder
¼ teaspoon salt
2 cups all-purpose flour, or 2¼ cups cake flour

AN 8- TO 12-CUP TUBE, TURK'S HEAD, OR BUNDT PAN

Heat the oven to 325°F. Grease the pan well.

Coarsely chop the chocolate with a knife or in a food processor. Scrub and dry one orange. With a vegetable peeler, remove the brightly colored part of the peel.

Squeeze the oranges and measure the juice. Add a little water or additional orange juice if needed to bring it up to ⅓ cup.

Put the orange peel and the sugar in a food processor and process until the peel is very finely chopped. (Instead of using a food processor, you may grate the unpeeled orange and add the peel to the sugar in the bowl.) The sugar will be damp. Scrape the sugar mixture into the bowl in which you will make the batter.

Add the butter and vanilla and beat with an electric mixer on high speed, until pale and fluffy.

Reduce the speed to medium. Add the eggs, 1 at a time, beating after each. Beat in the chopped chocolate, the baking powder, and salt. Scrape the sides of the bowl often.

With the mixer on low, mix in the orange juice. Sprinkle in the flour. Stir just until incorporated. Do not overmix.

Spread the batter (5 cups) evenly in the pan. Bake about 1 hour and 5 minutes. This cake is a little tricky to test for doneness because the cake tester usually comes up covered with hot melted chocolate. Remove the cake from the oven once a cake tester shows that it is *still just slightly damp inside.*

Cool the cake in the pan on a wire rack for 30 to 40 minutes. Loosen the edges and turn the cake out. For best flavor, store airtight 1 day at room temperature before serving or freezing.

PUMPKIN POUND CAKE

A lovely addition to a holiday table, but welcome any time of the year. Good solo or with Nutmeg-Honey Whipped Cream (page 118) or Pineapple–Golden Raisin Sauce (page 119).

15 tablespoons (2 sticks minus 1 tablespoon) unsalted
*   butter, at room temperature*
½ cup granulated sugar, or 1 cup confectioners' sugar
½ cup packed light brown sugar
2 teaspoons vanilla extract
4 large eggs, at room temperature
2⅓ cups all-purpose flour, or 2⅔ cups cake flour
1 teaspoon baking powder
1 teaspoon ground cinnamon
1 teaspoon ground nutmeg
½ teaspoon ground ginger
¼ teaspoon baking soda
¼ teaspoon salt
¼ teaspoon ground cloves
1 cup canned plain pumpkin (half a 16-ounce can)

SUGAR AND SPICE TOPPING
2 tablespoons granulated sugar
½ teaspoon ground cinnamon
½ teaspoon ground nutmeg

(continued)

A 9 × 5 × 3-INCH LOAF PAN

Heat the oven to 325°F. Grease the pan.

Beat the butter, sugars, and vanilla with an electric mixer on high speed, until pale and fluffy.

Reduce the speed to medium. Add the eggs, 1 at a time, beating after each.

Reduce mixer speed to low.

Beat in 1 cup of the flour, the baking powder, cinnamon, nutmeg, ginger, baking soda, salt, and cloves. Then add the pumpkin. The batter may look curdled.

When well blended, stir in the remaining flour until just incorporated. Do not overmix.

Spread the batter (5 cups) in the pan. Mix together the Sugar and Spice Topping ingredients and sprinkle on top.

Bake until a cake tester inserted in the center comes out clean, about 1 hour and 10 minutes.

Cool the cake in the pan on a wire rack for about 30 minutes. Loosen the edges and turn the cake out. Let cool completely. *Wrap airtight. Store at room temperature no longer than 12 hours.* After that refrigerate or freeze, or else the cake will spoil.

VARIATION

RAISIN PUMPKIN POUND CAKE

Use the same ingredients and pan as for Pumpkin Pound Cake (page 75), plus:

¾ cup dark raisins

Follow directions above, adding the raisins to the batter along with the pumpkin. Increase the baking time to 1 hour and 25 or 30 minutes, until the cake tests done, as described. Store as directed above.

VANILLA-BEAN VANILLA CAKE

12 PORTIONS

If you love vanilla, you'll love this sweet cake. It is petite—just about 1 inch high—but what it lacks in stature it makes up for in soothing, comforting vanilla flavor. Enjoy it with a small scoop of *vanilla* ice cream, or with slightly sweetened mashed strawberries. Sip espresso or a perfumey tea, such as Earl Grey or Lapsang souchong. But first, invest in a moist, good-quality vanilla bean. (Many vanillaphiles favor bourbon vanilla beans from Madagascar. Ask for them at spice or cookware stores.)

Use a springform pan if you have one; it eliminates the need to turn the cake upside down, disturbing the vanilla sugar topping. However, you can also line a 9-inch round cake pan with aluminum foil, leaving just enough foil extending over the edge so that you can lift out the foil and the cake with it.

1 vanilla bean
1 cup granulated sugar
12 tablespoons (1½ sticks) unsalted butter,
  at room temperature
4 large eggs, at room temperature
1 teaspoon baking powder
1 teaspoon vanilla extract
⅛ teaspoon salt
1¼ cups all-purpose flour, or 1½ cups cake flour

A 9- TO 9½-INCH SPRINGFORM PAN OR A 9-INCH ROUND CAKE PAN LINED
WITH FOIL (SEE ABOVE)

Heat the oven to 325°F. Grease the pan or the foil. Snip
tough ends off the vanilla bean and cut into ½-inch lengths.

Food processor method: Process the bean with the sugar for
5 minutes (yes, that long), until very finely chopped. Do not
open the processor until the sugar dust has settled. To remove
any remaining large chunks of vanilla bean, sift the sugar
through a strainer onto a piece of wax paper. The sugar may
be hot; let it cool for 4 or 5 minutes.

Blender method: Put the sugar in a blender and start the
machine. Gradually drop in the chunks of vanilla bean. (Keep
container closed as much as possible, to contain the cloud of
sugar.) When all is added, blend about 1 minute longer. Wait
until the sugar settles, then sift and cool as directed above.

To make the cake: Set aside 2 tablespoons of the vanilla
sugar for the topping. Mix the butter and the remaining vanilla
sugar with an electric mixer, then beat on high speed for
about 5 minutes, until pale and fluffy. Reduce the speed to
medium. Add the eggs, 1 at a time, beating after each. Turn the
mixer to low. Beat in the baking powder, vanilla, and salt. Add
the flour, about one third at a time, mixing only until blended.
Spread the batter (3½ to 4 cups) evenly in the pan. Bake 25
minutes. Moving the cake as little as possible, sprinkle the
reserved 2 tablespoons vanilla sugar over the surface. Continue to bake until the cake is a deep golden brown and a cake

tester inserted in the center comes out clean, about 15 minutes longer. (The sugar will change color, darkening slightly.)

Cool the cake in the pan on a wire rack for 15 to 20 minutes. Loosen the edges. Remove the springform sides and let the cake cool on the base, then loosen the bottom with a thin metal spatula and carefully slide the cake onto a plate. Or, lift the cake out of the pan by the foil. Carefully peel off the foil. Tightly wrapped, the cake keeps up to 1 week at room temperature; it also freezes well.

BROWN SUGAR–BROWN BUTTER–HAZELNUT POUND CAKE

10 TO 12 PORTIONS

Brown butter imparts a unique, rich, caramelly flavor to this cake, and the browning process turns the butter virtually into an oil. This cake is made very differently from most pound cakes, and as the technique involves cooking butter to a high temperature, just to be on the safe side, please invite small children and animals to leave the kitchen while you make the cake.

1 cup toasted hazelnuts or pecans (page 8)
16 tablespoons (2 sticks) unsalted butter
4 large eggs, at room temperature
1 cup packed dark brown sugar
1 teaspoon vanilla extract
¼ teaspoon salt
1 teaspoon baking powder
2 cups all-purpose flour

A 9 × 5 × 3-INCH OR AN 8½ × 4½ × 2¾-INCH LOAF PAN

Heat the oven to 325°F. Grease the pan.

(continued)

Finely chop the toasted hazelnuts or pecans with a knife or in a food processor.

Put the butter in a heavy 2- to 3-quart stainless steel saucepan over moderately high heat. Keeping one eye on the butter (once it melts, cooking time will be 5 to 6 minutes), crack the eggs into the bowl in which you will be making the batter. Add the sugar and beat with an electric mixer on high speed until thick and pale brown, about 4 minutes. Have ready a strainer and a glass 2-cup (or larger) measure. Now pay attention to the butter. A foam will appear on the surface and the butter will bubble merrily, big bubbles at first, then small ones, like a honeycomb. As the butter continues to cook, it will look crusty and awful but begin to smell wonderful, and the milk solids on the bottom of the pan will turn brown. If you have a candy or fat thermometer, use it. The butter is ready when it reaches 300°F. to 310°F., and looks clear and brown.

Remove the pan from the heat and pour the hot butter through the strainer into the cup measure. Then, with the mixer on medium speed, pour the hot butter—very carefully, so it doesn't splash—down the side of the bowl into the egg mixture in a steady stream, taking not more than 1 minute to add it all. Increase speed to high and continue to beat about 2 minutes, while adding the vanilla and salt.

With mixer on low, add the nuts and baking powder and beat about 15 seconds. Scrape the sides of the bowl. Add the flour, about ½ cup at a time, sprinkling it over the surface and not waiting until each amount is fully incorporated before you add the next. Scrape the sides of the bowl once or twice.

Spread the batter (4 cups) in the pan. Bake until a cake tester inserted in the center comes out clean, about 1 hour and 15 minutes. Cool the cake in the pan on a wire rack for 20 to 30 minutes. Loosen the edges and turn the cake out. Let cool completely. Store airtight a few hours or overnight at room temperature before serving or freezing.

TOASTED COCONUT AND ALMOND POUND CAKE

12 PORTIONS

This cake speaks for itself, but if you feel an irresistible urge to serve it with something, sliced fresh oranges and/or vanilla or butter pecan ice cream will fill the bill. There's lots of texture in this cake from the coconut and almonds.

1½ loosely packed cups sweetened shredded or flaked coconut
    (about 5 ounces)
1 cup whole almonds with skins still on (about 5 ounces)
12 tablespoons (1½ sticks) unsalted butter,
    at room temperature
2¼ cups confectioners' sugar, or 1¼ cups granulated sugar
1 teaspoon vanilla extract
¾ teaspoon almond extract
5 large eggs, at room temperature
1¼ teaspoons baking powder
¼ teaspoon salt
2¼ cups all-purpose flour, or 2⅓ cups cake flour

A 9 × 5 × 3-INCH LOAF PAN OR A 9 × 3-INCH SPRINGFORM PAN

Heat the oven to 350°F. Coarsely chop the coconut and almonds in a food processor. Spread on a large pan with sides. Bake about 15 minutes, stirring four or five times, until lightly browned. Cool completely. (Tip the mixture onto a cookie sheet or even the countertop to speed cooling.)

Reduce the oven temperature to 325°F. Grease the baking pan.

Beat the butter, sugar, and extracts with an electric mixer on high speed, until pale and fluffy. Reduce the speed to medium. Add the eggs, 1 at a time, beating after each. Beat in the baking powder and salt. Scrape the sides of the bowl.

With the mixer on low, add the cooled toasted nuts. Scrape the sides of the bowl. Add the flour and mix until just incorporated. Do not overmix.

Spread the batter (5 cups) evenly in the pan. Bake until a cake tester inserted in the center comes out slightly moist, but the cake is springy to the touch and shrinks from the sides of the pan, about 1 hour.

Cool the cake in the pan on a wire rack for about 30 minutes. Loosen the edges. Turn the cake out from the loaf pan; or remove the springform sides, slide a thin metal spatula under the cake, and gently slide it onto the rack. Let cool completely. For best flavor, store airtight 1 day at room temperature before serving or freezing.

PISTACHIO-GINGER
POUND CAKE

12 PORTIONS

Ginger brings out the subtle
flavor of the pistachios.

6 ounces (1¼ cups) shelled pistachio nuts (see Note)
3 ounces crystallized ginger
1 cup granulated sugar
16 tablespoons (2 sticks) unsalted butter,
  at room temperature
4 large eggs, at room temperature
1¼ teaspoons ground ginger
1 teaspoon baking powder
¼ teaspoon salt
2 cups all-purpose flour, or 2½ cups cake flour

A 9 × 5 × 3-INCH LOAF PAN

FOOD PROCESSOR

Heat the oven to 325°F. Grease the pan.

Put the shelled pistachios in a small saucepan of boiling water and boil 1 minute. Drain the pistachios and place on one half of a linen or cotton dish towel. Fold the towel over the nuts and rub to loosen the skins. Peel off the brown skins.

Reserve 1 or 2 pieces of crystallized ginger to decorate the top of the cake. Put the sugar and the remaining crystallized ginger in a food processor. Process 1 to 2 minutes, until the ginger is finely chopped. The sugar will be rather damp. Add about half the pistachios and process briefly to chop. Scrape the mixture into the bowl in which you plan to make the batter.

Add the butter and beat with an electric mixer on medium speed, until well blended. Increase the speed to medium-high and add the eggs, 1 at a time, beating after each, and scraping the sides of the bowl two or three times.

Beat in the ground ginger, baking powder, and salt. With the mixer on low, add the flour and the remaining whole pistachios. Scrape the sides of the bowl two or three times, and beat only until the flour is just incorporated. Do not overmix.

Spread the batter (5 cups) evenly in the pan. Draw the handle of a rubber spatula once lengthwise through the batter 1 inch deep. (This will bake into an attractive split.) Slice the reserved crystallized ginger thin, and scatter or arrange it on top of the batter.

Bake until a cake tester inserted in the center comes out clean, about 1 hour and 10 to 20 minutes.

Cool the cake in the pan on a wire rack for about 30 minutes. Loosen the edges and turn the cake out. Let cool completely. For best flavor, store airtight 1 day at room temperature before serving or freezing.

NOTE: You may be able to buy pistachios that have been peeled as well as shelled. If so, they are ready to add to the food processor and the cake.

FESTIVE POUND CAKE

Expect to find a creamy, moist center when you slice through the crusty, slightly sunken top of this delicate cake. Its fine grain and sweet flavor go especially well with a glass of Champagne and a few strawberries for a festive occasion. A mixer with two bowls or a sturdy portable one works well here.

16 tablespoons (2 sticks) unsalted butter,
  at room temperature
2 cups granulated sugar, or 4 cups confectioners' sugar
1 teaspoon vanilla extract
5 large eggs
½ teaspoon baking powder
2 cups all-purpose flour, or 2¼ cups cake flour

A 9 × 5 × 3-INCH LOAF PAN

Heat the oven to 325°F. Grease the pan.

Put the butter and all but about ¼ cup of the granulated sugar or ½ cup of the confectioners' sugar in a large bowl. Add the vanilla. Set aside.

Crack open each egg, letting the whites drop into a deep, narrow bowl or electric mixer bowl, and putting the yolks in a separate small dish.

Beat the egg whites with an electric mixer on high speed,

until soft peaks fold over when the beater is lifted. Sprinkle in the remaining ¼ cup granulated sugar or ½ cup confectioners' sugar and beat until the beaters leave a trail in the mixture.

Without washing the beaters, beat the butter and sugar on medium speed, until pale and fluffy. Slip in the yolks, 1 at a time, beating briefly after each. Beat in the baking powder and scrape the sides of the bowl. With mixer on low, add the flour and beat until almost incorporated. Scrape the sides of the bowl. Add a big spoonful of the egg whites and beat it in to lighten the mixture. Add the remaining egg whites and fold in with a rubber spatula, just until incorporated.

Scrape the batter (5 cups) into the pan and smooth the surface. Draw the handle of a rubber spatula once lengthwise through the batter ½ inch deep. (This will bake into an attractive split.)

Bake until the top is a light golden brown and a cake tester inserted in the center comes out clean, about 1 hour and 15 minutes. Cool the cake in the pan on a wire rack for 30 minutes. Loosen the edges and turn the cake out. Let cool completely. For best flavor, store airtight 1 day at room temperature before serving or freezing.

LEMON-MACE POUND CAKE

12 PORTIONS

$\mathbf{M}$ace is a very close relative of nutmeg—in fact it is the lacy brown wrap around the small oval nutmeg. The amount of mace specified is just right. To measure ⅛ teaspoon, fill and level off ¼ teaspoon. Then, with the point of a knife, "cut" the mace across the middle and scoot half back into the jar. This cake is excellent with Plum Sauce (page 121) and Raspberry-Blueberry Sauce (page 120).

2 large lemons
1¼ cups granulated sugar
16 tablespoons (2 sticks) unsalted butter,
  at room temperature
2 teaspoons vanilla extract
4 large eggs, at room temperature
1 teaspoon baking powder
¼ plus ⅛ teaspoon ground mace
¼ teaspoon baking soda
¼ teaspoon salt
2 cups all-purpose flour

A 9 × 5 × 3-INCH LOAF PAN

Heat the oven to 325°F. Grease the pan.

Scrub the lemons and pat dry. With a vegetable peeler, remove the brightly colored part of the peel and measure. You will need ⅓ cup lightly packed. Squeeze the lemons to make ⅓ cup juice.

Put the lemon peel and sugar in a food processor and process until the peel is very finely chopped. (Instead of using a food processor, you may grate the unpeeled lemons and add the peel to the sugar in the bowl.) The sugar will be very damp. Scrape the sugar mixture into the bowl in which you will be making the batter.

Beat the butter, the sugar mixture, and the vanilla with an electric mixer on high speed, until pale and fluffy.

Reduce the speed to medium. Add the eggs, 1 at a time, beating after each.

Beat in the lemon juice, baking powder, mace, baking soda, and salt (the batter will look curdled). Scrape the sides of the bowl often.

With the mixer on low, stir in the flour just until incorporated.

Spread the batter (5 to 6 cups) in the pan. Draw the handle of a spatula once lengthwise through the batter ½ inch deep. (This will bake into an attractive split.)

Bake until a cake tester inserted in the center comes out clean, about 1 hour and 5 to 10 minutes.

Cool the cake in the pan on a wire rack for about 30 minutes. Loosen the edges and turn the cake out. Let cool completely. For best flavor, store airtight 1 day at room temperature before serving or freezing.

SHIRLEY SARVIS'S FLORENTINE LOAF

12 PORTIONS

This may not be a cake you make for a party but, rather, one you make for a small gathering of appreciative friends. The cake has a crusty top that shatters when you cut it and it is deliciously wet in the middle. The raisins sink. But the taste is spectacular, like all food and wine writer Shirley Sarvis's recipes. Reducing the sugar to 2 cups will cure the texture "problem." But it also "cures" the moist center I love.

12 tablespoons (1½ sticks) unsalted butter,
  at room temperature
2⅔ cups confectioners' sugar
3 large eggs, at room temperature
⅓ cup yellow cornmeal
1 teaspoon vanilla extract
¼ teaspoon salt
½ cup golden raisins
1¼ cups cake flour, or 1 cup all-purpose flour
⅓ cup dark rum or sweet marsala wine

A 9 × 5 × 3-INCH LOAF PAN

Heat the oven to 325°F. Grease the pan. Line the pan with foil, letting it hang over the sides. Grease the foil.

Mix the butter and sugar in a large bowl with an electric mixer. When well blended, beat on high speed about 5 minutes, until pale and fluffy.

Reduce the speed to medium. Add the eggs, 1 at a time, beating after each. Add the cornmeal, vanilla, and salt. Beat to blend well. Scrape the sides of the bowl often.

With the mixer on low, stir in the raisins. Mix in about one third of the flour and half the rum or marsala. As soon as they are about halfway mixed in, mix in the remaining flour and rum or marsala. Scrape the sides of the bowl. Do not overmix.

Spread the batter (5 cups) evenly in the pan. Bake about 1 hour and 15 to 25 minutes. A sugary crust will form on top and a cake tester inserted in the center will come out with damp, sticky cake attached but not raw batter. Do not overbake.

Cool the cake in the pan on a wire rack for about 5 minutes. Loosen the edges, then let the cake cool completely in the pan. Lift the cake out of the pan by the foil. Carefully peel off the foil. For best flavor, store airtight 1 day at room temperature before serving or freezing.

CHIFFON CAKES

Because they are made with oil instead of butter, chiffon cakes are relatively easy to put together. Essentially, the flour and other dry ingredients are mixed in a large bowl. Then the wet ingredients—water, oil, honey—are mixed in, along with egg yolks when called for. You can do all this mixing by hand with a wooden spoon in a large bowl and save your electric mixer (a portable electric one works fine, here) for the egg whites. Lastly, the egg whites are beaten stiffly—slightly stiffer than for an angel food cake—and folded into the flour mixture.

Plan to make most of these cakes at least the day before you want to serve them because the flavors need that standing time to mellow and intensify. If you don't believe me, take a tiny piece from the bottom of a freshly baked and cooled cake and taste it. Compare it to the flavor a day or so later.

Chiffon cakes freeze well and take only an hour or two to thaw. Slice them while still frozen and they will thaw even faster.

ORANGE AND LEMON
NO-CHOLESTEROL OLIVE OIL
CHIFFON CAKE

16 PORTIONS

This has an absolutely delightful flavor and no one will guess that it is made with extra-virgin olive oil or that the egg yolks found in a traditional chiffon cake have been dispensed with. Do use extra-virgin or virgin olive oil; it makes a serious contribution to the overall flavor. The cake looks pretty sprinkled with confectioners' sugar before serving.

2 lemons
1 or 2 navel oranges
2 cups all-purpose flour
1½ cups granulated sugar
1 tablespoon baking powder
½ cup extra-virgin olive oil
1 cup egg whites (see page 7 if you need help)
½ teaspoon salt

A 10 × 4-INCH TUBE PAN (A REMOVABLE BOTTOM IS HELPFUL)

Heat the oven to 325°F. If the pan has a removable bottom, do nothing to it. If it does not, lightly grease the bottom (page 11). Line the bottom with wax paper or parchment paper cut to fit, and lightly grease the paper.

(continued)

Scrub and dry the lemons and oranges. Grate the colored part of the peel, taking care not to grate any bitter white part, until you have (loosely packed) 1 tablespoon grated lemon peel and 2 teaspoons grated orange peel (see Note). Juice the fruit and measure ½ cup orange juice and ¼ cup lemon juice.

Put the flour, 1 cup of the sugar, and the baking powder into a large bowl. Stir to mix well. Add the oil, fruit juices, and grated peel. Beat smooth with a wooden spoon.

Put the egg whites and salt in a deep narrow bowl and beat with an electric mixer on medium-high speed, until they lose their yellow cast, greatly increase in volume, and begin to turn very white.

While still beating, sprinkle in the remaining ½ cup of sugar, about 2 tablespoons at a time. Whites will become very thick and very white and the beaters will leave a deep trail.

Whisk or beat about one eighth of the whites into the flour mixture. With a large metal spoon or rubber spatula, fold or gently stir in the remaining whites.

When well blended, pour the batter (8 cups) into the pan.

Bake until golden brown, springy to the touch, and a cake tester inserted in the center of the cake comes out clean, 50 to 55 minutes.

Turn the pan upside down on a wire rack. If the cake has baked higher than the rim of the pan, turn the pan upside down onto a beer or soda bottle (the bottle goes in the hollow tube). Leave on countertop until cake is completely cold. Loosen the edges (and tube) with a knife. Turn out the cake, loosen and remove the pan bottom, or peel off the paper. Serve freshly baked, or wrap airtight and store 1 day at room temperature before serving or freezing.

NOTE: Instead of grating the peel you can remove the peel of the lemons and 1 of the oranges with a vegetable peeler. Put them into a food processor or blender with the 1 cup of sugar and process 3 or 4 minutes (yes, that long) until chopped as fine as possible. The sugar will be moist. Add it with the oil, not the flour. Be sure not to try to whip it with the egg whites, because the citrus oils will deflate them.

CHOCOLATE-ORANGE NO-CHOLESTEROL CHIFFON CAKE

16 PORTIONS

2 navel oranges
3 ounces semisweet chocolate
2 cups all-purpose flour
1½ cups granulated sugar
1 tablespoon baking powder
½ cup extra-virgin olive oil
1 cup egg whites (see page 7 if you need help)
½ teaspoon salt

A 10 × 4-INCH TUBE PAN (A REMOVABLE BOTTOM IS HELPFUL)

Heat the oven to 325°F. If the pan has a removable bottom, do nothing to it. If it does not, lightly grease the bottom (page 11). Line the bottom with wax paper or parchment paper cut to fit, and lightly grease the paper.

Scrub and dry the oranges. Grate the colored part of the peel, taking care not to grate any bitter white part, until you have (loosely packed) 4 teaspoons grated orange peel (see Note). Juice the oranges and measure ¾ cup.

Grate the chocolate or chop in a small food processor.

Put the flour, 1 cup of the sugar, the chocolate, and the baking powder into a large bowl. Stir to mix well. Add the oil, orange juice, and grated peel. Beat smooth with a wooden spoon.

Put the egg whites and salt in a deep narrow bowl and beat with an electric mixer on medium-high speed, until they lose their yellow cast, greatly increase in volume, and begin to turn very white.

While still beating, sprinkle in the remaining ½ cup of sugar, about 2 tablespoons at a time. Whites will become very thick and very white and the beater will leave a deep trail.

Whisk or beat about one eighth of the whites into the flour mixture. With a large metal spoon or rubber spatula, fold or gently stir in the remaining whites.

When well blended, pour the batter (7 to 8 cups) into the pan.

Bake until golden brown, springy to the touch, and a cake tester inserted in the center of the cake comes out clean, about 50 to 55 minutes.

Turn the pan upside down on a wire rack. If the cake has baked higher than the rim of the pan, turn the pan upside down onto a beer or soda bottle (the bottle goes in the hollow tube). Leave on countertop until cake is completely cold. Loosen the edges (and tube) with a knife. Turn out the cake, loosen and remove the pan bottom, or peel off the paper. Serve freshly baked, or store airtight 1 day at room temperature before serving or freezing.

NOTE: Instead of grating the peel you can remove the peel of the oranges with a vegetable peeler. Put it into a food processor or blender with the 1 cup of sugar and process 3 or 4 minutes (yes, that long), until chopped as fine as possible. The sugar will be moist. Add it with the oil, not the flour. Be sure not to try to whip it with the egg whites.

NO-CHOLESTEROL
CHIFFON SPICE CAKE

16 PORTIONS

2 cups all-purpose flour
1½ cups granulated sugar
1 tablespoon baking powder
1 teaspoon ground cloves
1 teaspoon ground cinnamon
¼ teaspoon freshly ground black pepper
¾ cup apple juice or cider
½ cup extra-virgin olive oil
1 tablespoon vanilla extract
1 cup egg whites (see page 7 if you need help)
½ teaspoon salt

A 10 × 4-INCH TUBE PAN (A REMOVABLE BOTTOM IS HELPFUL)

Heat the oven to 325°F. If the pan has a removable bottom, do nothing to it. If it does not, lightly grease the bottom (page 11). Line the bottom with wax paper or parchment paper cut to fit, and lightly grease the paper.

Put the flour, 1 cup of the sugar, the baking powder, cloves, cinnamon, and pepper into a large bowl. Stir to mix well. Add the apple juice or cider, the oil, and the vanilla. Beat smooth with a wooden spoon.

Put the egg whites and salt in a deep narrow bowl and beat with an electric mixer on medium-high speed, until they lose their yellow cast, greatly increase in volume, and begin to turn very white.

While still beating, sprinkle in the remaining ½ cup of sugar, about 2 tablespoons at a time. Whites will become very thick and very white and the beater will leave a deep trail.

Whisk or beat about one eighth of the whites into the flour mixture. With a large metal spoon or rubber spatula, fold or gently stir in the remaining whites.

When well blended, pour the batter (7 to 8 cups) into the pan.

Bake until golden brown, springy to the touch, and a cake tester inserted in the center of the cake comes out clean, about 50 to 55 minutes.

Turn the pan upside down on a wire rack. If the cake has baked higher than the rim of the pan, turn the pan upside down onto a beer or soda bottle (the bottle goes in the hollow tube). Leave on countertop until cake is completely cold. Loosen the edges (and tube) with a knife. Turn out the cake, loosen and remove the pan bottom, or peel off the paper. Serve freshly baked, or store airtight 1 day at room temperature before serving or freezing.

WALNUT-DATE CHIFFON CAKE

12 TO 16 PORTIONS

T he walnuts and dates usually form a layer on the bottom of the cake.

1 cup all-purpose flour
1 cup granulated sugar
1 teaspoon baking powder
½ teaspoon ground cardamom
¼ teaspoon salt
¼ teaspoon baking soda
One 8-ounce package pitted dates
1 cup walnuts, coarsely chopped
¼ cup vegetable or mild olive oil
¼ cup mild or dark molasses
3 large eggs

A 10 × 3-INCH ROUND CAKE PAN OR A 10 × 4-INCH TUBE PAN (A REMOVABLE BOTTOM IS HELPFUL)

Heat the oven to 325°F. If the pan has a removable bottom, do nothing to it. If it does not, lightly grease the bottom (page 11). Line the bottom with wax paper or parchment paper cut to fit, and lightly grease the paper.

In a large bowl, mix the flour, ¾ cup of the sugar, the baking powder, cardamom, salt, and baking soda. Stir with a wooden spoon to mix well.

Chop the dates, or cut them into small pieces with oiled

scissors; you should have just about 2 cups. Add the dates and the walnuts to the bowl and toss with your fingers to mix and coat with flour.

Add ½ cup water, the oil, and molasses. Separate the egg yolks from the whites (see page 7 if you need help), dropping the yolks into the oil and water and putting the whites into a deep narrow bowl. Stir the flour mixture until smooth and well blended.

Beat the egg whites with an electric mixer on medium-high speed until they lose their yellow cast, greatly increase in volume, and begin to turn very white.

While still beating, sprinkle in the remaining ¼ cup of sugar, about 2 tablespoons at a time. Whites will become very thick and very white and the beater will leave a deep trail.

Whisk or beat about one eighth of the whites into the flour mixture. With a large metal spoon or rubber spatula, fold or gently stir in the remaining whites.

Pour the batter (5 to 6 cups) into the pan. Bake until a cake tester inserted in the center comes out fairly clean but with no uncooked batter sticking to it, and the cake is springy to the touch, about 1 hour.

Turn the pan upside down on a wire rack until cake is completely cold. Loosen the edges (and tube) with a knife. Turn out the cake, loosen and remove the pan bottom, or peel off the paper. Store airtight 1 to 2 days at room temperature before serving or freezing.

KUMQUAT-ALMOND
CHIFFON CAKE

10 TO 12 PORTIONS

This small, moist cake is a great reason to rescue those festive little citrus fruits before they dehydrate in the fruit bowl.

*½ pound kumquats (about 2 cups or 24 kumquats), stems
    removed*

*1 cup almonds (blanched, unblanched, slivered, whatever,
    doesn't matter)*

2 cups granulated sugar

½ cup vegetable or mild olive oil

*5 large eggs, yolks and whites separated (see page 7 if
    you need help)*

2 teaspoons baking powder

¼ teaspoon baking soda

1½ cups all-purpose flour

A 10 × 4-INCH TUBE PAN (A REMOVABLE BOTTOM IS HELPFUL)

FOOD PROCESSOR

Put the kumquats in a small saucepan and cover with cold water. Bring to a boil. Cover and simmer 20 to 25 minutes over low heat, until the kumquats are tender when pierced. (This can be done a day or two ahead.) Drain, reserving ¼ cup cooking liquid, and cool the kumquats.

Heat the oven to 325°F. If the pan has a removable bottom, do nothing to it. If it does not, lightly grease the bottom (page 11). Line the bottom with wax paper or parchment paper cut to fit, and lightly grease the paper.

Put the almonds and 1½ cups of the sugar into a food processor and process for 1 to 2 minutes, until the nuts are very finely chopped.

Add the ¼ cup kumquat cooking liquid to the processor, along with the oil and egg yolks.

Remove any seeds from the kumquats, and drop the fruit into the food processor. Process until the kumquats are chopped fine. Sprinkle the baking powder and baking soda and then the flour over the surface. Process to mix in, scraping the sides of the bowl once or twice.

In a large bowl, beat the egg whites with an electric mixer on medium-high speed, until the whites lose their yellow cast, greatly increase in volume, and begin to turn white. While still beating, sprinkle in the remaining ½ cup sugar, about 2 tablespoons at a time. Whites will turn very white and glossy, and the beater will leave a deep trail.

Spread about one eighth of the beaten whites over the surface of the kumquat mixture. Turn the processor on/off four or five times to incorporate the whites.

Scrape the kumquat mixture into the bowl of whites and fold in just until blended. Scrape the batter (8 cups) into the pan. Bake until a cake tester inserted in the center of the cake comes out fairly clean—cooked but not raw batter clinging to it is okay—and the cake feels springy to the touch, about 1 hour and 15 minutes.

Place the pan on a wire rack and let cake cool completely. Loosen the edges (and tube) with a knife. Turn out the cake, loosen and remove the pan bottom, or peel off the paper. Store airtight 1 to 2 days at room temperature before serving or freezing.

COFFEE-HAZELNUT
HONEY CAKE

You can use pecans or almonds instead of hazelnuts, and ½ cup packed brown sugar instead of the granulated sugar and molasses. You may also replace the water and instant coffee granules with ½ cup of brewed espresso. Make this cake at least 2 days before you need it. The egg whites are not beaten separately as they are in most chiffon cakes.

2½ cups all-purpose flour
½ cup granulated sugar
1 tablespoon baking powder
½ teaspoon baking soda
¼ teaspoon salt
1 teaspoon ground cardamom
1½ cups golden raisins (7½ to 8 ounces)
1 cup toasted hazelnuts (page 8), coarsely chopped
2 tablespoons instant coffee granules
5 large eggs
1¼ cups honey (1 pound)
½ cup vegetable or mild olive oil
2 tablespoons mild or dark molasses

A 10 × 4-INCH TUBE PAN OR A 10 × 3-INCH ROUND CAKE PAN (A REMOVABLE BOTTOM IS HELPFUL)

(continued)

Heat the oven to 325°F. If the pan has a removable bottom, do nothing to it. If it does not, lightly grease the bottom (page 11). Line the bottom with wax paper or parchment paper cut to fit, and lightly grease the paper.

Put the flour, sugar, baking powder, baking soda, salt, and cardamom into a large bowl. Stir to mix well. Add the raisins and hazelnuts. Toss to coat with the flour.

Mix ½ cup water and the coffee and stir until coffee is dissolved. Add to the flour mixture along with the eggs, honey, oil, and molasses. Beat with an electric mixer or wooden spoon until well blended.

Scrape the batter (6 to 7 cups) into the pan. Bake until the cake feels springy to the touch and a cake tester inserted in the center of the cake comes out clean, 1 hour and 10 to 15 minutes.

Place the pan upside down on a wire rack to cool at least 30 minutes. Loosen the edges (and tube) with a knife. Turn out the cake, loosen and remove the pan bottom, or peel off the paper. Store airtight at least 2 days at room temperature before serving or freezing.

MOCHA CHIFFON CAKE

12 PORTIONS

Petite, but full of flavor.

¾ cup milk
3 ounces unsweetened chocolate, cut up
1 tablespoon instant coffee granules
4 large eggs
1 cup all-purpose flour
1½ cups granulated sugar
1½ teaspoons baking powder
¼ teaspoon salt
⅓ cup vegetable oil
1 tablespoon vanilla extract
Confectioners' sugar

A 10 × 4-INCH TUBE PAN (A REMOVABLE BOTTOM IS HELPFUL)

Put the milk, chocolate, and coffee granules in a heavy saucepan over very low heat. Heat, stirring occasionally, until the chocolate has melted. Remove from heat and let cool. (To hasten cooling, sit pan in cold water in the sink or in a bowl of ice water for a few minutes.)

Crack open the eggs, letting the whites drop into a deep narrow bowl and putting the yolks in a small dish. Let the whites come to room temperature (about 20 minutes).

Meanwhile, heat the oven to 325°F. If the pan has a removable bottom, do nothing to it. If it does not, lightly grease the bottom (page 11). Line the bottom with wax paper or parchment paper cut to fit, and lightly grease the paper.

Mix the flour, 1¼ cups of the sugar, the baking powder, and salt in a large bowl.

Add the oil, the yolks, and the vanilla to the cooled chocolate mixture. Add the chocolate mixture to the flour mixture and stir to blend well.

Beat the egg whites with an electric mixer on medium-high speed until the whites lose their yellow cast, greatly increase in volume, and begin to turn white. While still beating, sprinkle in the remaining ¼ cup sugar, about 2 tablespoons at a time. Whites will turn very white and glossy, and the beaters will leave a deep trail.

Beat about one eighth of the beaten whites into the flour mixture. Then gently stir or fold in the remaining whites with a rubber spatula or metal spoon.

Scrape the batter (6 cups) into the pan. Bake until a cake tester inserted in the center of the cake comes out clean, about 50 minutes to 1 hour.

Place the pan on a wire rack to cool for 30 minutes. Loosen the edges (and tube) with a knife. Turn out the cake, loosen and remove the pan bottom, or peel off the paper. Store airtight 1 to 2 days at room temperature before serving or freezing. Sift confectioners' sugar over the top before serving.

NEW YORK CARROT CAKE

Hazelnuts and ginger turn country mouse carrot cake into a small city slicker.

1½ to 2 cups peeled carrots cut in ½-inch lengths
2 tablespoons grated or diced, peeled fresh gingerroot
1 cup granulated sugar
½ cup vegetable oil
¼ cup orange juice or water
¼ cup mild molasses
3 large eggs
1 cup toasted hazelnuts (page 8)
1¼ cups all-purpose flour
1½ teaspoons baking powder
1 teaspoon ground cinnamon
½ teaspoon salt
⅓ cup golden raisins

A 10 × 4-INCH TUBE PAN (A REMOVABLE BOTTOM IS HELPFUL)

FOOD PROCESSOR

Heat the oven to 325°F. If the pan has a removable bottom, do nothing to it. If it does not, lightly grease the bottom (page 11). Line the bottom with wax paper or parchment paper cut to fit, and lightly grease the paper.

Put the carrots and ginger into a food processor and

process several seconds, until finely chopped.

Add ¾ cup sugar, oil, juice or water, and the molasses.

Crack open the eggs, letting the whites fall into a deep narrow bowl and adding the yolks to the processor. Process briefly to mix.

Add the hazelnuts and turn processor on/off four or five times to coarsely chop them. Scrape the sides of the bowl. Sprinkle the flour, baking powder, cinnamon, and salt over the surface; turn the machine on/off four or five times and then scrape the bowl sides.

Add the raisins. Turn on/off two or three more times to mix them in. Scrape bowl sides.

Beat the egg whites with an electric mixer on medium-high speed until they lose their yellow cast, greatly increase in volume, and begin to turn very white. Beat in the remaining ¼ cup sugar, about 2 tablespoons at a time. Whites will turn very white and glossy, and the beaters will leave a deep trail.

Spread about one eighth of the beaten whites on top of the mixture in the work bowl. Turn processor on/off three or four times to incorporate the whites.

Scrape the contents of the work bowl into the bowl of beaten whites and fold or gently stir with a rubber spatula or metal spoon, just until blended in.

Scrape the batter (6 cups) into the pan. Bake until the cake is springy to the touch and a cake tester inserted in the center comes out clean, about 1 hour. Place the pan on a wire rack to cool for 1 hour or longer. Loosen the edges (and tube) with a knife. Turn out the cake, loosen and remove the pan bottom, or peel off the paper. Store airtight 1 to 2 days at room temperature before serving or freezing.

TOPPINGS

CHOCOLATE WHIPPED CREAM

2 CUPS

2 ounces semisweet and 1 ounce unsweetened chocolate,
   or 3 ounces bittersweet chocolate
1 cup heavy (whipping) cream
1 tablespoon granulated sugar
½ teaspoon vanilla extract

Chop the chocolate, then melt it with 3 tablespoons water in a 1- to 2-quart heavy saucepan over low heat, stirring frequently until smooth. Remove from the heat and cool until the chocolate is cool to the touch but not cold.

Whip the cream with an electric mixer on high speed until it begins to thicken. Add the melted chocolate, sugar, and vanilla and whip until soft peaks form when the beater is lifted. Watch carefully so the cream doesn't turn into butter.

Serve right away or chill for up to 1 hour.

VARIATION

MOCHA WHIPPED CREAM
Prepare Chocolate Whipped Cream (above) as directed, adding ¼ teaspoon powdered instant espresso coffee to the cream along with the chocolate, sugar, and vanilla.

NUTMEG-HONEY
WHIPPED CREAM

ABOUT **2** CUPS

1 cup heavy (whipping) cream
1 tablespoon plus 1 teaspoon honey
⅛ teaspoon ground nutmeg

Whip the cream with an electric mixer on high speed until it begins to thicken. Add the honey and the nutmeg and continue whipping until soft peaks form when the beater is lifted.

Serve right away or chill for up to 1 hour.

PINEAPPLE–GOLDEN
RAISIN SAUCE

1½ CUPS

1 tablespoon unsalted butter
⅓ cup packed light brown sugar
⅓ cup cold unsweetened pineapple juice
1½ cups peeled, cored, and diced fresh pineapple
   (¼-inch dice)
⅓ cup golden raisins
1 teaspoon cornstarch

Melt the butter in a medium-sized nonstick skillet over moderate heat. Stir in the sugar and 1 tablespoon of the pineapple juice and cook until bubbly.

Add the diced pineapple and raisins to the sugar mixture, reduce the heat to low, and simmer about 8 minutes, stirring occasionally, until the pineapple is tender and translucent.

Mix the remaining pineapple juice with the cornstarch until smooth. Stir into the mixture in the skillet. Increase heat slightly and stir until boiling. Simmer 1½ to 2 minutes. Remove from heat. Serve warm.

RASPBERRY-BLUEBERRY SAUCE

2 CUPS

Wonderful with Lemon-Mace Pound Cake (page 90). Be sure to use a good-quality preserve.

2 cups fresh or unsweetened frozen raspberries
⅓ cup raspberry preserves or jam
2 tablespoons granulated sugar
1 cup fresh or frozen blueberries (small berries work better here)

Mix 1 cup of the raspberries, the preserves, ⅓ cup water, and the sugar in a medium-sized heavy saucepan (not uncoated aluminum). Bring to a boil over moderately high heat, mashing the raspberries with a wooden spoon. Boil 1 minute. Remove from heat.

Strain the raspberry mixture through a fine strainer suspended over a bowl, pressing down on raspberries to release juices. Discard the seeds.

Stir the blueberries and the remaining 1 cup raspberries into the hot raspberry syrup. Cover and let stand until cool. Refrigerate until ready to use.

PLUM SAUCE

1¼ to 1½ pounds ripe tart red plums, such as Santa Rosa
plums (about 8 small plums)
¾ cup granulated sugar (try ⅔ cup if plums are very sweet)
One 3-inch cinnamon stick, broken in half,
or ⅛ teaspoon ground cinnamon
Pinch of ground cloves

Halve and pit the plums. Cut each half into four or six wedges. You should have 3½ to 4 cups.

Mix all ingredients in a medium-sized heavy saucepan. Cover and bring just to a simmer over moderate heat, stirring every couple of minutes. The plums will release liquid that mixes with and dissolves the sugar.

Reduce heat to low and simmer 4 to 6 minutes, until the plums are hot and soft. Remove from heat. (Plums will continue to cook slightly.)

Remove the cinnamon stick. Serve sauce warm or chilled.

CARAMEL APPLES

Fabulous with one of the plainer cakes or with Brown Sugar Angel Food Cake (page 20).

3 tablespoons unsalted butter
⅓ cup packed dark brown sugar
1¼ pounds Granny Smith apples, peeled, cored, and
    cut into ¼-inch-thick wedges (about 4 cups)

Melt the butter in a large nonstick skillet over moderately high heat. Stir in the sugar and cook 1 to 2 minutes, stirring frequently until well blended and bubbly.

Add the apples to the sugar mixture and toss with two wooden spoons until well coated. Reduce heat to low, cover, and cook about 20 minutes, stirring every 4 or 5 minutes and pushing apples down into the syrup, until apples are tender and translucent.

Remove from heat. Serve warm.

SUPERB CHOCOLATE SAUCE

ABOUT 1½ CUPS

Try a small spoonful with Caramel-Coffee Angel Food Cake (page 26), with Miriam's Sour Cream Pound Cake (page 58), or Festive Pound Cake (page 88).

1 cup heavy (whipping) cream
6 ounces bittersweet or semisweet chocolate,
*   coarsely chopped*
2 tablespoons unsalted butter
1 tablespoon granulated sugar

Put all the ingredients in a medium-sized heavy saucepan. Stir over low heat until the chocolate is melted. Serve hot.

VARIATIONS

Add 1 tablespoon Cognac.
Add 1 teaspoon vanilla extract.

INDEX